Study Guide to Accompany
Papalia/Olds:

Human Development

Second Edition

Prepared by
DOUGLAS K. USELDING
University of South Dakota

for

P.S. Associates
Sterling, Massachusetts

McGraw-Hill Book Company
New York St. Louis San Francisco Auckland Bogotá Hamburg
Johannesburg London Madrid Mexico Montreal New Delhi Panama
Paris São Paulo Singapore Sydney Tokyo Toronto

Study Guide to Accompany
Papalia/Olds: HUMAN DEVELOPMENT
Second Edition
Copyright © 1981 by McGraw-Hill, Inc. All rights reserved.
Printed in the United States of America. No part of this publication
may be reproduced, stored in a retrieval system, or transmitted, in any
form or by any means, electronic, mechanical, photocopying, recording, or
otherwise, without the prior written permission of the publisher.

ISBN 0-07-048394-9

3 4 5 6 7 8 9 0 WHWH 8 9 8 7 6 5 4 3 2

This book was printed and bound by The WHITLOCK PRESS—Middletown, N.Y.

CONTENTS

PREFACE

There was a fashionable theory a few years back suggesting that, if you went to sleep with a tape recording of something you wanted to learn playing in the background, by morning you would have perfect recall of everything on the tape.

Well, it just isn't so. If learning were that easy, we would all be geniuses (and colleges would soon be out of business). There is no pat formula for learning, and there is no pat formula for mastering the information in Diane Papalia and Sally Olds's text, Human Development, Second Edition.

But we think this Study Guide will go a long way toward helping you understand the concepts, terms, and themes presented in the Papalia and Olds text. In fact, if you do the exercises contained in this guide in a careful and conscientious way, and pay special attention to the review materials provided in each chapter, then your chances of doing well in the course will be quite high indeed.

Why?

Because, for each chapter of the text, you are going to be told in advance what the most important ideas and facts in the chapter are and therefore what you should take time to learn. Then you will be given spaces in which to write out these very same ideas and facts on which you will later be tested. Next you will have an opportunity to review these facts and principles by means of simple practice exercises. You will also be given two Self Tests that may resemble the one your instructor will be giving you on the material presented in the chapter. And finally, you will be given an opportunity to apply what you have learned to the study of children.

Let's review these learning steps.

INTEGRATOR   So often, in so many of the texts you will read as a college student, the question, "Where does this chapter fit into the scheme of the whole text?" is never asked or answered. Chapters often appear as a loose federation: separate, equal, and unrelated. Here in the Integrator section of each chapter of the Study Guide, the chapter you are reading is placed in the context of human development as an ongoing process. The Integrator answers such questions as: How does this chapter relate to the previous chapter? What other chapters go into many of the same issues but use older or younger children as the basis for discussion? The Integrator may be considered part of the Overview, and it should be approached in the same way.

OVERVIEW   Within the dozen or so paragraphs that begin each chapter of your guide, the essential themes and issues discussed in the corresponding text chapter are presented. Each Overview is divided into sections, with each section covering a major section of the text. In addition, the key terms introduced in each section of the text are listed. It is highly recommended that you use 3x5 index cards to construct flash cards, listing each key term on one side of a card and its definition on the other. These flash cards will provide you with a very handy learning tool that will greatly assist you in both learning the items and testing your knowledge. Read the Overview before you start work on a chapter (to help you focus on the important points in the chapter) or after you have completed your reading of the chapter (to serve as a review and reinforcer of these important facts and principles). Either way-- or both ways--pay close attention to the Overview. It establishes the framework of the entire chapter.

LEARNING OBJECTIVES No ifs, ands, or buts: If you master these objectives plus any others your instructor may have given you, you have mastered the chapter. Mastering the objectives does not guarantee that you will remember everything the next day, but it does make it a lot more likely. You should try to complete each objective without referring to the text. Then look up the correct response only if you are stumped and need assistance.

MULTIPLE-CHOICE QUESTIONS   How well have you mastered the objectives? Self Test A serves as an index of your progress. If you perform well on it, go on to the Vignettes. (A score of 9 out of 10 is passing.) If you do not do well, continue by working through the Practice Exercises, then try your hand on Self Test B. If you reviewed the chapter carefully and diligently worked through the practice sections, you should score well this time. Answers to the Practice Exercises and the Self Tests are given at the back of the Study Guide.

PRACTICE EXERCISES   These exercises are designed to reinforce your comprehension of the learning objectives for the chapter. The exercises include a variety of formats, such as matching, true-false, word scramble, term finder, and completion. They are designed not only to emphasize critical material from each chapter but to be fun as well. One point must be emphasized about the completion exercises. In many cases, the answer you write in will not be the answer cited in the Answer Key at the back of the Study Guide. If you think your response is just as good as the one given in the Answer Key, check with the text for clarification. (A text page number appears after each answer for all exercises in the key.) You may do the Practice Exercises immediately after completing the Learning Objectives, or you may wait a few hours, days, or even weeks before you attempt them, thereby using the exercises to test your recall of the objectives and to reinforce your learning of them.

VIGNETTES   This final, brief section offers you an opportunity to apply your knowledge to some hypothetical situations. You should write down your responses on a separate sheet and then check these responses against the discussion of that topic in the text. Suggested answers are provided for most Vignettes in the Answer Key at the back of the Study Guide.

Sound easy? It is not. In fact, it's quite a bit of extra work. It demands that you put in at least an hour of additional effort after reading the text chapter. And, of course, it requires a commitment from you to follow faithfully the steps laid out in the Study Guide for mastering each chapter. The results should be worth the effort, however, and should enhance your appreciation of the goals set out by Papalia and Olds in designing and writing their text.

Good luck.

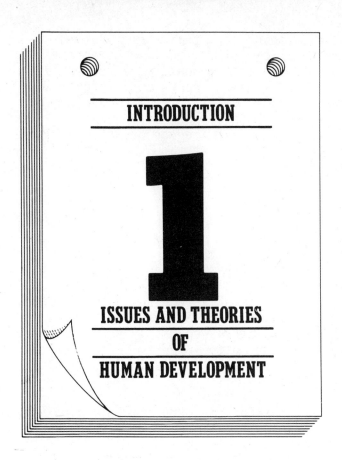

INTRODUCTION

1

ISSUES AND THEORIES
OF
HUMAN DEVELOPMENT

INTEGRATOR

You are about to begin the study of one of the youngest but most fascinating areas of psychology, human development. In chapters to come, we will review facts and theories about the physical, mental, personal, and social development that takes place during the life span of that most complex species, Homo sapiens. In Chapter 1 we will set the stage for this review by introducing the major theoretical positions and critical issues that have arisen during the history of developmental psychology. The chapter will end with a consideration of the methods used to study people and their development.

OVERVIEW

The Definition and History of the Study of Development

The first section of this chapter points out that development includes additions to behaviors that already exist, quantitative change, as well as complex "leaps" in functioning, qualitative change. Both such changes are lifelong processes, and the field of human development focuses not only on what changes occur but also on why they occur. This knowledge aids psychologists in achieving the two main goals of predicting future behavior and modifying problematic development.

1

The second section points out that the study of life span development
is a recent trend. Scientific, religious, economic, and social
advances culminated in the recognition of childhood as a special
developmental period, and the focus of interest expanded in the nine-
teenth and twentieth centuries to include adolescence and old age.
Concern with the entire life span was initiated by long-term growth
studies such as the Stanford Studies of Gifted Children, the Berkeley
Growth Study, the Oakland Growth Study, and the Fels Research Insti-
tute Study and is now a major facet of developmental psychology.

Key terms in this section:

quantitative change   goals in developmental psychology
qualitative change   life span development

Aspects and Periods of Life Span Development

As a person develops, there is continuing complex interaction among
his or her physical, intellectual, and personality growth. These
three aspects are considered separately for convenience, but each
is intimately dependent on the others. Change in interpersonal
interaction provides a case in point in demonstrating the complex
nature of development.

The text divides the life span into the following eight stages:
(1) the prenatal period, (2) infancy, (3) the preschool period,
(4) the school years, (5) adolescence, (6) young adulthood, (7)
mature adulthood, and (8) aging adulthood. The authors emphasize,
however, that these are arbitrary divisions. There are significant
individual differences among people, due in part to differing social
and economic backgrounds. Thus, within any given stage, people vary
widely in their development.

Key terms in this section:

interpersonal interaction   individual differences

Principles of Development

Despite individual differences, the following principles apply to
all developmental changes and can help us interpret information.

1. Although psychologists talk about average ages at which behaviors
    develop, people vary widely in their rate of development. People
    pass through developmental stages in the same order but not at
    the same speed.

2. There are times, called critical periods, when certain environ-
    mental events have their greatest impact on development.

3. Development is an ordered, organized process. The well-defined
    path is evident in simple to complex, general to specific,
    cephalocaudal, proximodistal, and cognitive stage development.

4. Different types of development are important at different times.

Key terms in this section:

rate vs. order of development	cephalocaudal development
critical periods	proximodistal development
simple to complex development	cognitive stage development
general to specific development	

Models and Theories of Human Development

Psychologists have adopted differing perspectives or models of developmental change. These models are associated with specific theories of development, each with its own strengths and weaknesses.

1. The mechanistic perspective or mechanical mirror model. This view of development sees it as primarily quantitative and focuses on people's reactions to their environment as they develop in a gradual, continuous fashion. Behaviorists such as Ivan Pavlov and B. F. Skinner emphasize the effects of classical (or respondent) and operant (or instrumental) conditioning. These systems are excellent examples of theories based on a mechanistic perspective. Social learning theorists such as Jerome Kagan and Albert Bandura also adopt a mechanistic view but emphasize imitation as a method of learning.

2. The organismic perspective emphasizes quantitative and qualitative changes in behavior and focuses on the individual's active role in producing these changes. Development is seen as a discontinuous process occurring in a set of qualitatively differing stages. Jean Piaget's cognitive theory is a prime example of this view. According to Piaget, one's view of the world, or schema, develops through assimilation and accommodation via a set sequence of stages. The four main stages of cognitive development are the sensorimotor, preoperational, concrete operational, and formal operational stages. Lawrence Kohlberg's theory of moral development also uses the organismic perspective. Moral reasoning is theorized to proceed through premoral, conventional, and postconventional stages as people develop.

3. The psychoanalytic perspective sees development as based upon continual internal conflict between natural impulses and societal constraints. The psychosexual theory of Sigmund Freud is a prime example of this model. In this view personality is a conflict among id, ego, and superego which changes its focus of concentration as the individual passes through the oral, anal, phallic, latency, and genital stages of psychosexual development. Adult personality is seen as influenced by success in conflict resolution or fixation at earlier stages. Erik Erikson has proposed eight stages of development in which the conflict to be resolved incorporates not only internal forces but external ones. At each stage the individual must resolve a social crisis to

develop a sense of trust, autonomy, initiative, industry, identity, intimacy, generativity, or integrity.

4. The humanistic perspective of development incorporates a most positive view of human nature. People are considered to be basically neutral or good. Problems in development are seen as the result of damage to the developing self. While not a true developmental theory, Abraham Maslow's conceptualization of a hierarchy of needs ranging from physiologic needs to needs for safety, belongingness and love, esteem, and ultimately self-actualization typifies the humanistic approach. Charlette Buhler's postulation that achieving self-fulfillment during the phases of childhood, adolescence and young adulthood, young and middle adulthood, mature adulthood, and old age is a humanistic approach to development.

Key terms in this section:

mechanistic perspective
  (mechanical mirror model)
continuous development
classical (respondent)
  conditioning
operant (instrumental)
  conditioning
social learning theory
organismic perspective (organic
  lamp model)
schema
assimilation
accommodation
sensorimotor stage
preoperations stage
concrete operations stage
formal operations stage

moral development
premoral
conventional morality
postconventional morality
psychoanalytic perspective
oral stage
anal stage
phallic stage
latency stage
genital stage
id
ego
superego
humanistic perspective
Maslow's hierarchy of needs
self-fulfillment

The Influences of Heredity and Environment

The relative contribution of genetic inheritance and environmental forces in determining the course of development is embodied in the nature versus nurture controversy. While both are clearly important, the tabula rasa approach has had its followers in the past. Today the issue is not which is important but rather to what extent both are important. The relative contribution of each varies. For physical development and physiologic traits, identical twins tend to be more concordant than fraternal twins. For intelligence, the heredity and environment interaction is much more complex and integrated. Certain personality traits may have genetic components such as emotionality, hyperactivity, behavior traits, and some personality pathologies labeled schizophrenia. The influence of genetic versus environmental factors in development is measured through use of twin studies, adoption studies, consanguinity studies, selective breeding

4

studies, animal studies and studies comparing parental practices.

Key terms in this section:

tabula rasa	twin studies
physiologic traits	adoption studies
concordance	consanguinity studies
hyperactivity	selective breeding
schizophrenia	parental practice studies

Methods for Studying People

The various methods for studying people fall into three major categories. The naturalistic studies depend upon pure observation in
relatively natural settings. Used for normative purposes, these
methods include baby biographies, naturalistic observation, and
time-sampling. The clinical studies emphasize thorough exploration
of small numbers of people and include the clinical method and the
interview method. Experimental studies emphasize systematic change
of an independent variable and careful measure of changes in the
dependent variable. The use of experimental group and control group
comparisons is a powerful experimental procedure. Comparison of the
correlational nature of naturalistic studies and the causal nature
of experimental studies is also useful.

There are two major methods for collecting data. The longitudinal
design provides accurate information about the process of development but is subject to bias and practice effects. The cross-
sectional design is efficient and avoids practice effects but is
subject to cohort effects. A blending of the two major methods into
a cross-sequential design overcomes some problems but is itself
complicated and expensive.

Key terms in this section:

naturalistic studies	experimental and control groups
normative	correlational nature of methods
baby biography	replicability of experiments
naturalistic observations	longitudinal and cross-sectional
time-sampling	design
clinical studies	bias
clinical method	cohorts
interview method	cross-sequential design
experimental method	
independent and dependent variables	

Basic Ethical Issues

The study of human development must be conducted in a manner which
reflects sensitivity to several basic ethical concerns. These
include preservation of individual right to privacy, right to truth,

right to informed consent and right to self-esteem. These issues
are greatly emphasized in fetal research, research with the elderly,
and research relating to social concerns.

Key terms in this section

right to privacy	informed consent
self-fulfilling prophecy	right to self-esteem
right to truth	

LEARNING OBJECTIVES

1. The study of human development focuses on the quantitative and
   qualitative ways in which people change over time. Identify the
   differences between quantitative and qualitative changes in
   behavior. (p. 2)

2. Summarize the three phases in the history of the study of human
   development. (pp. 5-8)

3. Cite four important factors which influenced the emergence of
   the concept of "childhood" as a period that is distinctly
   different from "adulthood." (pp. 5-8)

   a.

   b.

   c.

   d.

4. Explain the relationships among physical, intellectual, and
   emotional development. (pp. 8-9)

6

5. List the six chronological periods of the human life span. (pp. 9-10)

6. Identify four general principles of development that help us interpret and organize information. (pp. 11-13)

   a.

   b.

   c.

   d.

7. Describe the basic view of people proposed by each of the following perspectives. (pp. 13-19)

   a. Mechanistic perspective

   b. Organismic perspective

   c. Psychoanalytic perspective

   d. Humanistic perspective

8. Explain the following terms as they are used in Piaget's theory of cognitive development. (p. 15)

   a. Schema

   b. Assimilation

   c. Accommodation

9. Identify the five stages of development proposed in Freud's psychosexual theory. (pp. 16-17)

10. Outline the social crises associated with each of Erikson's eight stages of development. (p. 17)

    a.

    b.

    c.

    d.

    e.

    f.

    g.

    h.

11. Define the nature-nurture controversy. Explain why it is impossible to say that development is the result of only one of these factors. (pp. 19-21)

12. List three ways to study the effects of heredity on behavior. List three ways to study the effects of environment on behavior. (pp. 22-23)

Heredity	Environment
a.	a.
b.	b.
c.	c.

13. Summarize briefly what the evidence suggests about the interaction of heredity and environment in shaping each of the following. (p. 23)

    a. physiological traits

b.   intelligence

c.   personality

d.   behavior traits

e.   schizophrenia

14.   Describe the major advantages and disadvantages of each of the
      following research methods.   (pp. 29-33)

a.   Naturalistic studies

b.   Clinical studies

c.   Experimental studies

15.   Describe the main strengths and weaknesses of the following
      data-collection methods.   (pp. 33-34)

a.   Longitudinal method

b.   Cross-sectional method

c.   Cross-sequential method

16.   Discuss the ethical issues involved in doing research with
      people.   Identify four rights of people who are research

subjects. (pp. 34-37)

17. Discuss the ethical issues involved in doing research with fetuses, the elderly, and minority groups. (pp. 34-39)

SELF TEST A

Circle the letter of the choice that best completes each item.

1. The difference in ability between a language-proficient 4-year-old and a 2-year-old who cannot yet talk is an example of: (a) qualitative development; (b) quantitative development; (c) continuous development; (d) cephalocaudal development.

2. Prior to the seventeenth century: (a) children were regarded as miniature adults; (b) the elderly were the only group given special attention; (c) childhood was viewed as an especially important developmental period; (d) adolescents were treated as children rather than as maturing adults.

3. The principle of individual differences in development means that: (a) every person is different and norms are impossible; (b) people pass through stages of development in varying order and speed; (c) development is a continuous process throughout the life span; (d) people differ widely in their rate of development.

4. If a woman contracts measles during her first three months of pregnancy, it can have serious consequences for the developing fetus. Contracting the disease during the last month of a pregnancy will not affect the young infant. This fact demonstrates the concept of: (a) proximodistal development; (b) critical period; (c) prenatal contagion; (d) simple to complex development.

5. "People are basically reactive and their development is the result of conditioning by the environment." This statement reflects a(n) _____ perspective of development. (a) humanistic (b) organismic; (c) mechanistic; (d) psychoanalytic.

6. According to Freud, if a child's needs are not met or if they are overindulged at a particular stage: (a) the superego will develop; (b) fixation may occur; (c) crises will be resolved; (d) the id-ego conflict will be settled.

7. John is in the process of setting specific well-defined goals for himself. According to Buhler, John is most probably a(n): (a) elderly man; (b) mature adult; (c) man in his late 20s; (d) 14-year-old adolescent.

8. A psychologist is studying the genetic basis of musical talent by testing all living members of a particular family to see if closeness of relationship affects the degree to which family members exhibit similar levels of talent. The psychologist is conducting a(n): (a) consanguinity study; (b) twin study; (c) experimental study; (d) cross-sequential study.

9. An advantage of the experimental method is that: (a) it overcomes cohort effects; (b) many facets of development can be studied at one time; (c) it establishes clear correlation between variables but not cause-effect relationships; (d) it is easier to replicate.

10. A major ethical concern in research which tests minor children is that permission to participate given by an adult may violate the child's: (a) right to truth; (b) right to informed consent; (c) right to privacy; (d) right to self-esteem.

PRACTICE EXERCISES

Word Scramble

Unscramble the ten items. Then arrange the circled letters to complete the sentence below.

1. _ _ _ _ _ _ _ _ Ⓐ _

   A A L T U B   A R A S

   The idea that people are born as "blank slates."

2. _ _ _ _ Ⓞ _ _ _ _ _ _ _

   U O D I N L A L N G I T

   Experimental design which gives information about the process of development.

3. _ _ _ _ _ Ⓞ _ _ _ _ _ _ _

   H A C L O C E P D A U L A

   Principle which says that physical development starts in the head area and proceeds downward.

4. _ _ Ⓞ _ _ _ _ _ _
   A   L   C   L   I   S   S   A   C

Conditioning associated with Pavlov.

5. _ _ _ _ Ⓞ _ _ _ _ _
   C   M   O   R   I   S   I   G   A   N

Model which emphasizes qualitative and quantitative development.

6. _ _ _ _ _ _ _
   H   A   P   I   C   L   L

Psychosexual stage in which concern is focused on genital stimulation.

7. _ _ Ⓞ _ _ _ _ _
   R   M   A   L   R   E   P   O

Level of moral reasoning characterized by desire to reap rewards.

8. _ _ _ _ _ _ _ _ _ _ Ⓞ _ _
   O   P   S   C   H   R   E   H   A   N   I   I   Z

Personality abnormality with some genetic basis.

9. _ _ _ _ _ _
   H   T   C   O   O   R

Effect which is a major problem in cross-sectional studies.

10. _ _ Ⓞ _ _ _ _ _   _ _ _ _ _ _ _
   F   D   I   O   R   N   M   E   N   S   C   O   T   N   E

Basic right that must be preserved in psychological research.

The emphasis today is on a _ _ _ _ _   _ _ _ _ approach to development.

True-False

Circle T if the statement is true, F if the statement is false.

T F   1.   Sudden "leaps" in functioning are characteristic of qualitative changes.

T F   2.   Two major goals of developmental psychologists are developing norms and predicting future behavior.

T F   3.   Physical, intellectual, and personality development
          occur at different rates and at different times within
          a single person and thus do not greatly affect one
          another.

T F   4.   Norms are useful even though there are wide individual
          differences in development.

T F   5.   Development proceeds generally from the general to the
          specific and from the simple to the complex.

T F   6.   Piaget's is a prime example of a theory based on the
          mechanistic perspective of development.

T F   7.   The order or Freud's psychosexual stages of development
          is oral, anal, genital, latency, phallic.

T F   8.   According to Maslow, the ultimate human need is self-
          actualization.

T F   9.   The syndrome of hyperactivity has been shown to have no
          genetic basis.

T F 10.   In longitudinal designs, practice effects are a major
          problem.

Completion

Supply the words or phrases that best complete these sentences.

1. Changes in height and weight are examples of _____
   change, whereas acquisition of skill in walking is an example

   of _____ change.

2. Although norms are available to describe average development,

   it is important to remember that there are many _____

   _____ in people's development.

3. A(n) _____ in development is a time
   when a given event will have its greatest impact.

4. Development that begins in the central midline portion of the
   body and proceeds out toward the peripheral portions is termed

   _____ development.

5. _____ theorists see developmental changes as

being quantitative and view people as reactive rather than

initiating. _____ theorists view changes in behavior as being both quantitative and qualitative and emphasize the active role of the individual.

6. The consideration of whether heredity or environment plays the more important role in development is called the _____-_____ controversy.

7. When researchers look at people in their normal habitats without intervening in any way, they are using _____ studies. These studies provide us with data on average times that behaviors occur among normal people, or _____ information.

8. Diaries or journals describing the day-to-day changes in the behaviors of a particular child are called _____.

9. In an experimental study, researchers manipulate a(n) _____ variable to observe its effects on a(n) _____ variable.

10. In a psychological study, teachers were told that certain children in their classes were intellectually gifted. In fact, these children then showed tremendous gains in their IQ scores.

This is an example of how a(n) _____ - _____ _____ might occur and shows that violation of the right of _____ can have rather serious effects.

SELF TEST B

Circle the letter of the choice that best completes each item.

1. Which of the following is not a general principle of development? (a) There are wide variations in rate of development across individuals. (b) Certain facets of development are subject to critical periods. (c) Different types of development are important at

different times. (d) Development within an individual will follow group norms of development.

2. Behaviorists such as Skinner, Watson, and Pavlov adhere to the: (a) organismic perspective of development; (b) mechanical mirror model of development; (c) organic lamp model of development (d) humanistic perspective of development.

3. According to Freud, the order of critical development stages is: (a) oral, latency, anal, phallic, genital; (b) oral, anal, phallic, genital, latency; (c) oral, anal, phallic, latency, genital; (d) anal, oral, phallic, genital, latency.

4. Erikson proposes that the first crisis the developing individual must face involves the development of a sense of: (a) trust; (b) identity; (c) generativity; (d) autonomy.

5. Charlotte Buhler proposes that, at each stage of development, a person must achieve: (a) autonomy; (b) esteem; (c) identity; (d) self-fulfillment.

6. Arguments over the relative importance of heredity and environment are collectively termed the: (a) life-span approach to development; (b) nature-nurture controversy; (c) consanguinity debate; (d) relative formulation argument.

7. A psychologist is systematically mating research animals to see if she can produce a genetically more intelligent strain of animal. She is using a: (a) twin study approach; (b) consanguinity study approach; (c) selective breeding study approach; (d) genetic mapping study approach.

8. Piaget is noted for having used the _____ method when developing his theory of cognitive development. (a) correlational; (b) clinical; (c) experimental (d) time sampling

9. A psychologist tests the effectiveness of a new reading program by testing the reading skills of a third-grade class and a fifth-grade class at the beginning and at the end of the first school semester. This psychologist is using a: (a) cross-sequential design; (b) cross-sectional design; (c) longitudinal design; (d) time-sampling design.

10. Research with the elderly poses a unique ethical question, because the elderly: (a) are senile and may not understand the experiment; (b) are near death and represent a special population; (c) in nursing homes may feel pressured to take part in experiments; (d) believe it is their duty to be subjects in experiments.

VIGNETTES

1.   You and a friend have just returned from a university production
of <u>Pygmalion</u>.   You saw Liza Doolittle transformed from a rough,
crude woman into a charming one.   Your friend says that such a thing
could never happen because people are programmed genetically to be
the way they are at birth.   How would you respond?   What is the other
extreme argument you could propose?

2.   In Charles Dickens's <u>Oliver Twist</u>, children are portrayed largely
as victims and as miniature adults.   What types of social, economic,
and religious advances have we made that would make such treatment
seem cruel and unlawful today?

3.   It has been argued that watching television causes children to
be more violent.   What type of evidence would you require in order
to be convinced that this is true?

BEGINNINGS

2

PRENATAL DEVELOPMENT
AND
BIRTH

INTEGRATOR

In Chapter 1 you encountered a long-standing issue among developmental psychologists--the nature-nurture controversy. In this chapter you will learn about specific ways that heredity can influence human traits. You will also see, however, that even prenatally the environment has tremendous impact on how those hereditary traits are expressed. This heredity-environment interaction will be a continuing theme in chapters to come.

As we examine the growth of the human fetus we will see the four basic principles of development at work. For example the embryonic stage is certainly a critical period for the developing child. Prenatal growth is both quantitative and qualitative with different kinds of development being more crucial at differing times. Finally the principles of cephalocaudal and proximodistal development are clearly illustrated in Table 2-1.

The chapter ends with a discussion of birth. Perhaps no event is equal to birth as a physical and psychological milestone in the life of parents and child. As the premiere event of life span development, birth marks the starting point of all we will discuss in remaining chapters.

OVERVIEW

Fertilization and Mechanisms of Heredity

The prenatal period is a time of numerous complex and important biological developments. This period is initiated when a spermatozoon
produced by the male testes joins an ovum released during ovulation
from one of the female's ovarian follicles. This joining normally
takes place in the Fallopian tubes as the ovum travels toward the
uterus and meets sperm that have passed through the cervix. It is
important to note that even though every individual possesses many
sex cells, or gametes, only one sperm is needed to fertilize an egg.

Uniting of a single sperm and an ovum to create a zygote is the first
step in the mechanism of heredity. Sperm and egg each contain
twenty-three chromosomes which carry genetic information on segments
of DNA molecules called genes. Of the twenty-three pairs of chromosomes each person receives, one pair will determine the person's
gender; this pair are called sex chromosomes. A child's sex is
determined by the joining of an ovum with either a gynosperm or an
androsperm. Information on nonsex chromosomes, called autosomes, can
be transmitted to males and females equally.

The genetic patterns associated with fraternal (dizygotic) and identical (monozygotic) multiple births are discussed. Whether a single
child or several children are created, there are four possible patterns of genetic transmission of traits. In autosomal dominant inheritance the allele for the dominant trait is paired with a recessive
trait allele. The phenotype associated with such a genotype will
reflect the dominant trait in 75 percent of the cases. When a person's genotype is composed of both dominant and recessive alleles,
they are said to be heterozygous. If only dominant or recessive
alleles are present, they are considered homozygous. When traits are
based upon multiple allele pairs, the method of inheritance is very
complex.

In autosomal recessive inheritance, two recessive genes must be inherited, one from each parent. Blue eyes are transmitted in this
way. Sex-linked inheritance refers to traits, other than gender,
which are determined by genes on the sex chromosomes. Color blindness is a good example of such a trait. Mendel's work on independent
segregation helps us to understand the complex hereditary patterns
in multifactor inheritance.

Key terms in this section:

prenatal period   follicles
spermatozoon   Fallopian tube
testes   uterus
ovum   cervix
ovulation   gametes

gynosperm vs. androsperm

zygote

chromosome

DNA

gene

sex chromosome

autosome

dizygotic twins vs. monozygotic
    twins

autosomal dominant inheritance

recessive trait vs, dominant
    trait

alleles

phenotype vs. genotype

heterozygous vs. homozygous

multiple allele

autosomal recessive inheritance

sex-linked inheritance

independent segregation

multifactor inheritance

Chromosomal Abnormalities, Genetic Counseling, and Diagnosis

Genetic transmission can at times yield a child who is afflicted with
abnormal traits. A number of such conditions are reviewed. These
are: (1) Down's syndrome, a well-known genetic abnormality resulting
in mental retardation; (2) Klinefelter's syndrome, which affects
males who possess the Barr body and require treatment with testosterone to treat some of the symptoms; (3) XYY syndrome, which also
affects males and is discussed in relation to Klinefelter's syndrome
and normal males; conditions affecting only females include (4)
Turner's syndrome and (5) XXX syndrome.

Genetic conditions such as anencephalia and those just described have
led to the increased use of genetic counseling. Sophisticated genetic
investigation using karyotypes and other tests helps counselors
determine the mathematical chances of a couple bearing a normal child.
Genetic counseling is used before a child is even conceived. Even
after conception, the possible existence of birth defects in an unborn
fetus can be diagnosed using amniocentesis, AFP level in the mother's
blood, ultrasound, fetoscopy, or electronic fetal monitoring.

Key terms in this section:

anencephaly

Down's syndrome

Barr body

testosterone

Klinefelter's syndrome

XYY syndrome

Turner's syndrome

XXX syndrome

karyotype

amniocentesis

AFP level

ultrasound

fetoscopy

electronic fetal monitoring

Prenatal Development

This major section describes some of the biological changes that occur
during prenatal development. Prenatal development can be divided
into three major stages. While it is almost impossible to fix the
exact age of a conceptus and many use rough estimates of menstrual age
and fertilization age, still these three stages serve as useful guidelines and describe the sequence but not the timing of prenatal
development.

During the germinal stage, the zygote begins rapid cell division and forms a blastocyst which enters the uterus from the Fallopian tube. The blastocyst will differentiate into the embryonic disk which will eventually form three layers: ectoderm, endoderm, and mesoderm. The blastocyst also contributes to the developing placenta, umbilical cord, and amniotic sac. Toward the end of the germinal stage, the trophoblast of the blastocyst (its outer layer) produces threadlike structures that penetrate the uterine lining and achieve implantation two weeks after fertilization. Once implanted, the cell mass is called an embryo.

The embryonic stage lasts about six weeks during which time major body systems and organs develop. Thus the embryonic stage or first trimester of a pregnancy represents a critical period in that prenatal environmental influences can have their most marked impact.

The fetal stage, which lasts from the eighth week until birth, is initiated by the appearance of the first bone cells. At this point, the developing child becomes a fetus. This period is one of continuing growth and development and is marked by several milestone events. Quickening at four months, the appearance of lanugo at five months along with definite sleep-wake cycles, and the development of lie are such milestones.

Termination of a pregnancy before a fetus is capable of surviving outside the womb can occur through either spontaneous abortion or induced abortion. If a fetus develops to term, it will spend its time as a very active passenger.

Key terms in this section:

conceptus	amniotic sac
menstrual age	trophoblast
fertilization age	embryo
germinal stage	trimester
blastocyst	embryonic stage
embryonic disk	fetal stage
ectoderm	fetus
endoderm	quickening
mesoderm	lanugo
placenta	lie
umbilical cord	spontaneous and induced abortion

The Prenatal Environment

The prenatal environment plays a crucial role in determining the extent to which the fetus's genetic traits will be expressed. Numerous environmental factors can have pronounced effects on prenatal development. Experience with cretins points to an important role for maternal nutrition in affecting the fetus; however, the evidence, except in extreme cases such as malnutrition, is contradictory as to the level of importance of the mother's diet.

The thalidomide tragedy, which resulted in hundreds of babies born with phoncomelia, underscores the potential impact of maternal drug intake on prenatal development. A large list of potentially hazardous drugs is reviewed with special attention given to the potential teratogenic risks of: (1) hormones such as oral contraceptives and diethylstilbestrol (DES), (2) smoking, which has recently been identified as a potentially harmful practice for pregnant women, (3) abuse of alcohol, which can have serious consequences leading to fetal alcohol syndrome (FAS), and even with moderate use by the mother carries increased risks for the developing fetus, (4) use of marijuana, which has not been shown conclusively to have effects beyond those of smoking in general, and (5) LSD and addictive drugs, which have clearer relationships to spontaneous abortion, fetal addiction, and disruption of normal fetal development.

Other influences on prenatal development include maternal disease such as rubella or venereal disease, incompatibility of blood type due to Rh factor, use of toxic chemicals in the environment, radiation resulting in mutations, and defects transmitted by the father.

Key terms in this section:

cretin   diethylstilbestrol (DES)
thalidomide   fetal alcohol syndrome (FAS)
phoncomelia   Rh factor
teratogenic risk

The Birth Process

While it is not yet known what triggers the uterus to contract to begin the birth process, the event itself progresses through three overlapping phases.

The first stage of labor is the longest lasting on average of twelve to twenty-four hours. The major process in this phase is dilation or a widening of the cervix. The second stage, which lasts about 1½ hours, begins with the baby entering the vaginal canal, head first, and ends with the birth. During the third stage the placenta and umbilical cord are expelled.

Different methods of childbirth have been proposed and each has its advantages and drawbacks. Those which employ medication ease the mother's discomfort but may have deleterious effects on the child. Alternative procedures include Lamaze's prepared childbirth and LeBoyer's birth without violence.

Major birth complications include cesarean delivery and low birthweight babies. The term premature has been dropped in favor of the more descriptive terms preterm and small-for-date. The exact effects of low birthweight are not clearly known; however both low birthweight and birth trauma have, in general, adverse effects on the newborn. In general, the more difficult a delivery, the greater the risk of anoxia, and the greater the potential damage.

Key terms in this section

dilation
medicated delivery
prepared childbirth
birth without violence
cesarean delivery

low birthweight infant
premature vs. preterm vs. small-
    for-date infants
birth trauma
anoxia

LEARNING OBJECTIVES

1. Briefly describe the sequence of events that occurs during the
    process of fertilization. Explain how sex is determined and
    how multiple births occur. (p. 44)

2. Describe the relationships among chromosomes, genes, and
    DNA. (pp. 46-47)

3. List and briefly describe four patterns of genetic transmission.
    Mention at least one trait that is transmitted via each
    pattern. (pp. 48-52)

    a.

    b.

c.

d.

4. Describe the genetic pattern and phenotypic traits associated with each of the following conditions. (pp. 52-55)

   a. Down's syndrome

   b. Klinefelter's syndrome

   c. XYY syndrome

   d. Turner's syndrome

   e. XXX syndrome

5. State the purpose of genetic counseling, and identify six diagnostic techniques used in detecting prenatal birth defects. (pp. 55-58)

   Purpose:

   Techniques:

   a.

   b.

   c.

   d.

e.

f.

6. Describe the evidence related to the relative importance of each of the following prenatal factors. (pp. 64-71)

    a. Maternal diet

    b. The Pill

    c. DES

    d. Tobacco smoking

    e. Marijuana

    f. LSD

    g. Addictive drugs

    h. Maternal disease

    i. Rh factor

    j. Radiation

    k. Birth defects transmitted by the father

7. List the three major stages of prenatal development and their main characteristics. (pp. 58-59)

   a.

   b.

   c.

8. Describe some possible causes of spontaneous abortion. (p. 63)

9. Describe the three stages that usually occur during the birth process. (pp. 72-73)

   a.

   b.

   c.

10. Compare the advantages and disadvantages of medicated delivery, cesarean delivery, natural childbirth, and birth-without-violence techniques. (pp. 73-75)

11. Describe some of the effects that low birthweight and birth trauma can have on the early development of the child. (pp. 75-77)

SELF TEST A

Circle the letter of the choice that completes each item.

1. Sperm and ova are examples of: (a) zygotes; (b) spermatozoon; (c) gametes; (d) autosomes.

2. John and Harry are twins who share the exact same genetic makeup. John and Harry are: (a) dizygotic twins; (b) monozygotic twins; (c) fraternal twins; (d) phenotypic siblings.

3. Karla has blue eyes. She inherited her eye color from her mother and father who also have blue eyes. Karla is _____ for eye color. (a) heterozygous; (b) dizygotic; (c) homozygous; (d) dominant.

4. Red-green color blindness is a trait transmitted by a pattern called: (a) autosomal dominant inheritance; (b) autosomal recessive inheritance; (c) independent inheritance; (d) sex-linked inheritance.

5. An extra X chromosome can produce a condition known as: (a) Klinefelter's syndrome; (b) Down's syndrome (c) Turner's syndrome; (d) XYY syndrome.

6. The zygote begins rapid cell division and forms into a blastocyst during the: (a) germinal stage; (b) embryonic stage; (c) fetal stage; (d) last trimester.

7. The placenta: (a) covers and protects the developing fetus; (b) protects the fetus from the effects of drugs; (c) delivers oxygen and nourishment to the fetus via the umbilical cord; (d) filters the blood of the fetus.

8. Cigarette smoking by pregnant women: (a) has beneficial effects on the developing fetus; (b) tends to increase the likelihood of a low-birthweight baby; (c) has no known effects on the developing fetus; (d) tends to decrease fetal heart rate.

9. Mary is in the delivery room in the process of giving birth to her first child. She has fully dilated and her child's head is just visible in the vaginal canal. Mary is in the: (a) first phase of childbirth; (b) second phase of childbirth; (c) third phase of childbirth; (d) fourth phase of childbirth.

10. When Joanna was born, she entered a warm room with soft lighting. After delivery, she was laid on her mother's abdomen and then transferred to a warm bath. Joanna was born using: (a) medicated delivery; (b) birth-without-violence technique; (c) natural or prepared childbirth; (d) cesarean delivery.

PRACTICE EXERCISES

Term Finder

```
A J O Q U L T R A S O U N D M P
E L V U I S M O D E R A P E R P
D W L A X I N O G Y T E S E L B
G O G E O Q N A E R A S E C C M
E M Y U L U C V C A S D A T O O
N S O L M S R E N R U T I O D D
A G N I N E K C I U Q V X D I B
K A S S X O N W I E T T B E Y I
A M N I O C E N T E S I S R E P
R O M T I B K C L Y Q S S M O F
Y S R O C D L K C M V I L T L A
O L E V G Y N O S P E R M A I L
T E T N A F T S E F K O M X G J
Y A E D B S M J N L F X O I T O
P E R A A N J X E L M N N D H L
E F P L S D O I G O A N N F G E
P R B V T H A L I D O M I D E C
```

Clues to the words hidden among the letters follow. The words may read forwards, backwards, up, down, or diagonally. Draw a circle around each word as you find it, and then write it beside the clue.

1. _____ Segments of DNA

2. _____ X-carrying sperm creating a female zygote

3. _____ Different forms of a gene

4. _____ XO syndrome affecting females

5. _____ A photographic display of chromosomes used

in genetic counseling

6. _____ Drawing and analysis of amniotic fluid for diagnosis of birth defects

7. _____ Use of sound waves to diagnosis prenatal conditions

8. _____ Fluid-filled sphere of cells floating freely in the uterus before implantation

9. _____ Layer of embryonic disk destined to become outer skin, nails, hair, teeth, and brain

10. _____ Fetal kicking movements often felt by a pregnant mother in her fourth month

11. _____ Tranquilizer which causes birth defects

12. _____ Type of infant who has been born too early

13. _____ Type of delivery which involves abdominal surgery

14. _____ Oxygen deprivation during birth

15. _____ Type of childbirth promoted by Dr. F. Lamaze

Completion

Supply the words or phrases that best complete these sentences.

1. Life begins when a(n) _____ cell from a male unites

   with a(n) _____ cell from a female, usually in the

   _____ _____. The single cell that is formed

   in this fertilization process is called a(n) _____.

2. Every human cell has twenty-three pairs of _____
   which carry the hereditary information of the individual.

   Twenty-two of these pairs are called _____, while the
   remaining pair, which determines a child's sex, is called the

   _____ _____.

3. When an organism is _____ for a particular trait, the

alleles for that trait are identical. If the alleles for a

trait are not the same, the organism is _____ for that trait.

4. The fact that some traits are transmitted separately is called

    _____ _____.

5. A chromosomal abnormality which produces mental retardation and altered physical traits, and which is related to increased

    maternal age, is called _____ _____.

6. Material which is found in the nucleus of the female cell but

    not in that of a male is called a(n) _____ _____.

7. Males who have a chromosomal configuration of XXY have

    _____ _____, which is sometimes treated

    by the administration of _____.

8. During the _____ stage of prenatal development, the zygote undergoes rapid cell division. In this stage, a thickened

    cell mass called the _____ forms, from which the baby will develop. Also, three nurturing and protec-

    tive organs, the _____, the _____

    _____, and the _____ _____, are formed at this time.

9. When a conceptus is expelled from the uterus prior to the time

    that it can survive outside the womb, a _____

    _____ is said to have occurred. Most of these occur

    in the first _____ of pregnancy.

10. Children who are slow in physical, motor and intellectual development and who are born to mothers who have been drinking

    heavily might be displaying a _____ _____ _____.

True-False

Circle T if the statement is true, F if the statement is false.

T F 1. Combining of a dominant gene and a recessive gene is the basis of autosomal dominant inheritance.

T F 2. John and Mary have quite different genotypes for hair color; it therefore follows that their phenotype will also be different.

T F 3. After fertilization, the zygote experiences rapid cell division and forms a fluid-filled cell mass called a trophoblast.

T F 4. Ultrasound represents a noninvasive technique for fetal diagnosis.

T F 5. The only difference between a preterm infant and a small-for-date infant is the child's weight.

T F 6. There is no evidence that tobacco smoking affects a developing fetus.

T F 7. During the third stage of the birth process, the placenta and umbilical cords are expelled.

T F 8. Oral contraceptives represent no teratogenic risk if taken before conception.

T F 9. Data indicate that the use of general anesthesia during birth may adversely affect the infant for up to one year.

T F 10. Data indicate that birth trauma always results in prolonged, lifelong loss in abilities such as reading, perceptual skills, and social competence.

SELF TEST B

Circle the letter of the choice that completes each item.

1. The cell that results from the fertilization of an ovum by a sperm is called a(n): (a) allele; (b) spermatozoon; (c) zygote; (d) gamete.

2. If both parents contribute the gene for blue eye color, their child will have blue eyes. This is an example of: (a) autosomal dominant inheritance; (b) autosomal recessive inheritance; (c) sex-linked inheritance; (d) multiple allele inheritance.

3. Segments of hereditary material that are carried on rod-shaped particles in every human cell are called: (a) chromosomes; (b) genes; (c) autosomes; (d) ova.

4. If two ova are each fertilized by two different sperm, the result will be: (a) monozygotic twins; (b) dizygotic twins; (c) a spontaneous abortion; (d) autosomal dominant inheritance.

5. John has just been born. At the point of his conception, his mother's ovum was joined by a(n): (a) follicle; (b) androsperm; (c) gynosperm; (d) sex chromosome.

6. Which of the following is true about low-birthweight babies? (a) They are more likely to be smaller, but intellectual functioning is not affected. (b) They are usually full-term infants whose parents are small in stature. (c) The more severely premature they are, the more severe are the deficits they show. (d) They exhibit clear deficiencies which they rarely overcome.

7. If a person displays a recessive trait in his phenotype, he must be _____ for that trait in his genotype. (a) homozygous; (b) heterozygous; (c) dominant; (d) autosomic.

8. The most organs of the body are formed during the _____ stage of prenatal development. (a) germinal; (b) embryonic; (c) fetal; (d) postnatal.

9. The portion of the embryonic disk that will eventually become the digestive and respiratory systems is the: (a) ectoderm; (b) endoderm; (c) mesoderm; (d) trophoblast.

10. A method of childbirth where mothers are trained to make new breathing and muscular responses to sensations of uterine contractions is called: (a) prepared childbirth; (b) birth without violence; (c) sensitivity training; (d) cesarean delivery.

VIGNETTES

1. In a recent article in a national magazine, the area of genetic engineering was discussed. The general view expressed stressed the potential dangers in our increasing skill in genetic diagnosis and manipulation. What might be some of the dangers and advantages in our increasing skill?

2. While working as a volunteer doctor's aide, you meet a young woman who has just discovered that she is pregnant. She is delighted and excited about her first pregnancy and willing to talk about her future. Seeing you in your blue doctor's-aide jacket, she strikes up a conversation by asking what types of things she might do to help care for herself and her unborn child. What might you suggest?

3. A school acquaintence has just told a group of friends that his aunt has given birth to a "mongoloid" child. He knows the child will be retarded, because the doctor tested the child's blood and found strange cells. What is wrong with your friend's information?

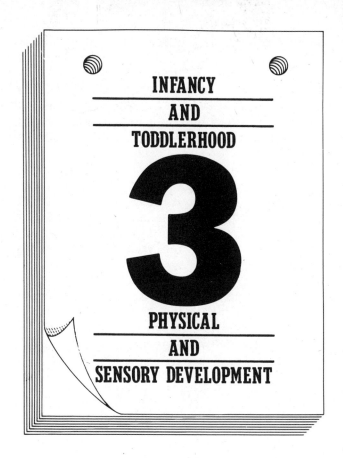

INFANCY
AND
TODDLERHOOD

3

PHYSICAL
AND
SENSORY DEVELOPMENT

INTEGRATOR

In Chapter 2, we considered human development during the prenatal period leading to the event of birth. At the point of birth, a unique individual begins to learn about and to affect persons and things in the world around. The capacity to affect and learn about the world rests upon the physical and sensory capacities. Everything a child knows about the world comes through the sensory systems. The cognitive personality and social skills to be discussed in upcoming chapters all depend ultimately on these basic abilities.

OVERVIEW

The Neonate: Physical Appearance, State, Body Systems, and Sensory Systems

The first sections describe the physical appearance, body systems, state, and sensory capacities of the neonate. The two- to four-week neonatal period begins at birth. The newborn is on the average 20 inches long and weighs 7 pounds. Additional prominent physical features often found include lanugo, vernix caseosa, fontanels, and excretion of meconium. The Apgar Scale is used to assess the newborn's condition one minute and five minutes after birth. The average score of 7 reflects normal appearance, grimace, pulse, activity, and respiration.

At birth, the infant's circulatory, respiration, gastrointestinal, and temperature-regulation systems must take over the supply of essential needs previously supplied by the prenatal environment. Anoxia and physiologic jaundice are examples of failure to make a smooth transition.

Infants vary in state and can be described as exhibiting: (1) regular sleep, (2) irregular sleep, (3) drowsiness, (4) alert inactivity, or (5) waking activity or crying. The state of the infant provides information about the infant's environmental responding and greatly influences parent behavior. Great individual differences exist among infants.

Infants have immature but remarkably effective sensory capacities. Visual skill in depth perception using the visual cliff and studies on visual preferences are examples of such capacities. Wide ranges of development are also seen in studies of hearing, smelling, tasting and feeling pain.

Key terms in this section:

neonatal period	physiologic jaundice
lanugo	meconium
vernix caseosa	state
fontanels	depth perception
Apgar Scale	visual cliff
anoxia	visual preference

Physical and Motor Development of Infants

Wide variations exist in the ages at which children develop certain physical skills. Nonetheless some general developmental trends are evident. During their first three years, babies grow markedly in size and experience large changes in body proportions. Several factors, including genetics, home environment, or prolonged illness, can influence physical growth. Breast feeding versus bottle feeding has been examined as a potentially critical factor. Generally, the quality of social interaction during feeding is possibly as important as the nourishment delivery system. Obesity is a major health problem for American children. It seems related to social class and may carry over into adulthood.

Motor development, the ability of the child to do things with his or her body, is very orderly. It is differentiating and integrative as it proceeds from the simple to the complex. This development begins as reflex behavior. There are numerous such reflexes, some of which are listed in Table 3-4. These are soon replaced by increasing mastery of voluntary movements. Milestones in such mastery are noted in head control, sitting, rolling over, prewalking locomotion (via crawling, hitching or scooting, bear-walking, and creeping) standing, walking, and grasping. Special attention is given to development of eye-hand coordination, which seems to progress through four major stages: (1) static visual exploration, (2) active and repeated visual exploration, (3) initiation of grasping and/or manipulation, and (4) refinement and extension.

The process of motor development is a matter of some controversy. Bower has raised questions about repetitive processes in motor development. Cross-cultural differences may exist in children's motor development. Toilet training represents a practical situation in which motor development is of great concern to parents.

Key terms in this section:

obesity   hitching (scooting)
motor development   bear-walking
differentiating development   creeping
integrative development   eye-hand coordination
reflexive behavior   repetitive processes
crawling

Sudden Infant Death Syndrome (SIDS)

The last section discusses the Sudden Infant Death Syndrome (SIDS) (also known as "crib death"). A leading cause of infant death, this condition is still a mystery with many possible causes being examined. Monitoring devices which signal periods of apnea have been used with high-risk infants, but such devices may cause more problems in their use.

Key terms in this section:

Sudden Infant Death Syndrome   apnea
    (SIDS)

LEARNING OBJECTIVES

1. Describe the physical characteristics of the average normal neonate. (p. 84)

2. Briefly describe changes that occur in each of the following systems during the neonatal period. (pp. 85-86)

Respiratory system

Gastrointestinal system

Temperature-regulation system

3. Name and describe the child's behavior in five classes of
   state. (p. 86)

   1.

   2.

   3.

   4.

   5.

4. Describe evidence that infants can see depth and demonstrate
   visual preferences at an early age. (pp. 88-90)

5. Describe the early capacities of neonates for each of the following behaviors. (p. 90)

    1. Hearing

    2. Smelling

    3. Tasting

    4. Feeling Pain

6. Discuss briefly the factors that influence the physical growth of the infant. (p. 92)

7. State some of the advantages that breast feeding has over bottle feeding. (pp. 93-94)

8. Explain why obesity in infancy can be a problem. (pp. 95-96)

9. Name and define two general processes that are involved in motor development. (p. 96)

10. Name and describe eight basic reflexes exhibited by newborns. (p. 97)

    1.

    2.

    3.

    4.

    5.

    6.

    7.

    8.

11. Explain the function of reflex behaviors and tell why some of them drop out of the infant's repertoire. (p. 97)

12. List seven motor skills considered as milestones in develop-
    ment and briefly describe the average ages and types of skills
    associated with each. (pp. 98-100)

    1.

    2.

    3.

    4.

    5.

    6.

    7.

13. List and describe four major stages of eye-hand coordination.
    (pp. 100-101)

    1.

    2.

3.

4.

14. Summarize Bower's argument about the discontinuity of motor development. (pp. 101-102)

15. Tell how the environment can retard motor development. (p. 102)

16. Tell how environmental influences can accelerate motor development. (p. 103)

17. Discuss the factors that are involved in successful toilet training. (pp. 103-104)

18. Explain the significance of cross-cultural differences in motor development. (pp. 104-106)

19. Define the term Sudden Infant Death Syndrome, and give some of its hypothesized causes. (pp. 106-107)

SELF TEST A

Circle the letter of the choice that completes each item.

1. The oily protective covering that covers the newborn at birth is called: (a) fontanels; (b) vernix caseosa; (c) lanugo; (d) witch's milk.

2. The series of tests used immediately after birth to determine the viability of the newborn is called the: (a) newborn assessment scale; (b) Bayley scale; (c) Apgar scale; (d) newborn viability scale.

3. Infants die from _____ more than from any other single cause. (a) respiratory problems; (b) circulatory problems; (c) gastrointestinal problems; (d) physiologic jaundice.

4. Harold is 1 week old. His eyes are open and he is quietly looking around the room. Harold's state is probably one of: (a) alert inactivity; (b) irregular sleep; (c) waking activity and crying; (d) drowsiness.

5. Studies using the visual cliff show that infants will see the illusion of depth by the age of: (a) 1 week; (b) 4 weeks; (c) 3 months; (d) 6 months.

6. Jane is a normal 2-month-old. Based upon her age we might expect her to prefer to look at: (a) her mother's expressionless face with eyes open; (b) a bull's-eye; (c) her mother's expression-

41

less face with eyes closed; (d) a picture of a face with only one eye.

7. A neonate who is held under his arms so that his feet just touch a flat surface will probably show the: (a) walking reflex; (b) tonic neck reflex; (c) rooting reflex; (d) Moro reflex.

8. Voluntary direct movements are possibly due to increased _____ control. (a) subcortical; (b) cortical; (c) reflexive; (d) sensory.

9. According to Bower, a behavior that apparently disappears and then reappears in the infant's repertoire of motor skills is: (a) the Moro reflex; (b) the Babinsky reflex; (c) eye-hand coordination; (d) sucking behavior.

10. The leading cause of death among infants aged 1 month to 1 year is: (a) Sudden Infant Death Syndrome; (b) "passive smoking"; (c) apnea; (d) anoxia.

PRACTICE EXERCISES

Completion

Supply the words or phrases that best complete these sentences.

1. The period from birth to four weeks is called the __neonatal__ period.

2. The average newborn baby is __20__ inches long and weighs __7__ pounds.

3. At birth, some newborns have a covering of fuzzy hair called __lanugo__, and all possess an oily protective coat of __vernix__ __caseosa__.

4. The newborn has several places on the head where the bones have not grown together. These soft spots are called __fontanels__.

5. Very soon after delivery, the newborn is assessed medically by the __Apgar__ __scale__, which measures five factors-- __appearance__, __pulse__, __grimace__,

42

_____activity_____, and _____respiration_____.

6. The newborn's sensory abilities to _____see_____, _____hear_____, _____smell_____, and _____taste_____ are all functioning at birth.

7. Physical differences between well-cared-for and poorer children show up in the _____first_____ year.

8. Involuntary behaviors exhibited by the infant are called _____reflex_____ _____. The brief appearance of some of these reflects the _____subcortical_____ control of the infant nervous system.

9. When an infant moves along in a sitting position, he is said to be _____scooting_____.

10. Successful attempts to toilet-train children are related to their _____maturational_____ level.

Matching

In the blank to the left of each definition, write the letter that indicates the term defined.

__i__   1. Soft areas on a newborn's skull
__j__   2. Scale used to evaluate newborns
__f__   3. Apparatus used to measure newborn's depth perception
__h__   4. State with eyes closed and irregular breathing
__g__   5. State with eyes closed; some body activity
__c__   6. Reflex elicited by stroking a newborn's cheek
__a__   7. Reflex elicited by stroking a newborn's foot
__d__   8. Period in which newborn stops breathing
__e__   9. Condition of lack of oxygen during birth
__b__   10. Major nutritional problem of American children

a. Babinsky   d. apnea
b. obesity   e. anoxia
c. rooting   f. visual cliff

g. drowsiness
h. irregular sleep

i. fontanels
j. Apgar

True-False

Circle T if the statement is true, F if the statement is false.

(T) F 1. The neonatal period is marked by a transition from intrauterine life to an independent existence.

T (F) 2. The typical Apgar score is 10.

T (F) 3. The newborn's gastrointestinal system excretes vernix caseosa during the first couple of days after birth.

(T) F 4. An infant is in the waking-activity state when her eyes are open and she is reacting to external stimuli.

T (F) 5. Newborns cannot see at birth.

T (F) 6. Infants do not feel pain until one to two weeks after birth.

T (F) 7. As long as the mother-child relationship is good, there are no advantages to breast feeding.

(T) F 8. Motor development proceeds from the simple to the complex through differentiation and integration of motor skills.

(T) F 9. Reflexes represent subcortical control of behavior.

(T) F 10. Practice has been shown to have beneficial effects on the development of walking skills.

(T) F 11. The average infant can stand with help at 8 months.

(T) F 12. The third stage of eye-hand coordination involves visual guiding of reaching behavior.

T (F) 13. Since motor development is based on genetic programs which simply mature, the environment cannot retard motor development.

T (F) 14. Data suggest that African infants exhibit slower motor development than the average Western baby.

(T) F 15. Crib death is a popular name for Sudden Infant Death Syndrome.

SELF TEST B

Circle the letter of the choice that completes each item.

1. Which of the following statements is accurate regarding physical development in infancy? (a) Hereditary factors are solely

44

responsible for the infant's body size. (b) Environmental factors such as nutrition are primarily responsible for the infant's physical size. (c) Heredity and environment interact to shape the course of physical development. (d) All infants tend to develop about equally during the first twelve months.

2. Marylou was lying quietly with her eyes closed and breathing regularly, but now her breathing has become more irregular and some slight muscle twitches can be seen. Marylou has passed from a state of _____ to a state of _____. (a) drowsiness, alert inactivity; (b) regular sleep, apnea; (c) regular sleep, irregular sleep; (d) irregular sleep, drowsiness.

3. Dennis (1960) found that, in Iranian institutions, infants in the deprived institutional environment showed: (a) marked motor retardation which persisted through school age; (b) some motor retardation, but "caught up" by school age; (c) no retardation of motor ability; (d) accelerated motor development which slowed with age.

4. A study wherein infants were given extended practice in using the walking reflex showed that: (a) They walked earlier than infants who had not received this practice. (b) They walked later than infants who had not received this practice. (c) They walked at the same age as infants who had not received this practice. (d) The walking reflex does not drop out as other reflexes do.

5. The feeding method that is best to use with an infant is: (a) bottle feeding; (b) breast feeding; (c) not as important as the quality of the mother-child relationship; (d) cereals and soft foods.

6. The later toilet training is begun: (a) the slower the child learns; (b) the faster the child learns; (c) the more likely it is that the child will suffer emotional upset; (d) the more difficult it is to break "bad habits."

7. Two-week-old Margi lies on her back and looks to the right. Her right arm is extended and she looks something like a fencer. Margi is exhibiting the: (a) tonic neck reflex; (b) Moro reflex; (c) Darwinian reflex; (d) Babinsky reflex.

8. At age 11 months, Richard would get around by "crawling" on his hands and feet. This prewalking locomotion technique is called: (a) crawling; (b) bear-walking; (c) creeping; (d) scooting.

9. African babies, when compared to norms based on white, Western infants, tend to exhibit: (a) precocious verbal skills; (b) re- tarded verbal skills; (c) precocious motor skills; (d) precocious verbal and motor skills.

10. The cessation of breathing for brief periods is called:
(a) anoxia; (b) apnea; (c) SIDS; (d) physiologic jaundice.

VIGNETTES

1. Imagine that you are taking a speech class. You are assigned
to prepare an impromptu speech on the topic: "The effectiveness
of programs to help premature infants." If you have but two
minutes for the speech, what will you say?

2. A friend who is training to be a nurse tells you that newborn
infants cannot hear, see, smell, or taste at birth. What would
you say in reply?

3. A girl you know is five months' pregnant and is very upset
about trying to choose between breast versus bottle feeding. Her
mother is pressuring her into breast feeding, but she is uncertain
about whether she wants to use that method. At the same time, she
feels very guilty about not breast feeding. She has come to you
for advice. What would you say?

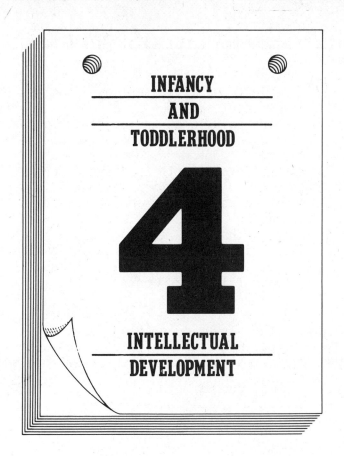

INFANCY AND TODDLERHOOD

4

INTELLECTUAL DEVELOPMENT

INTEGRATOR

In Chapter 3, we learned that infants undergo remarkable growth in
physical skill and have impressive sensory abilities for monitoring
and interacting with the world. With these abilities, the child
begins to learn and reason about the world. He begins to display
the intellectual capacities which will continue to develop throughout the life span. We will continue to study this development in
Chapters 6, 8, 10, 12, 14, and 16, and we will see how later skills
are founded upon the early stages of intellectual growth.

OVERVIEW

Piaget's Theory of Cognitive Development

Early intellectual functioning has many aspects, including cognitive
functioning, learning, and the acquisition of language. The Swiss
psychologist, Jean Piaget, has proposed a comprehensive theory of
one of these aspects, cognitive development. Piaget proposes that
children develop an internal representation of the world by integrat-
ing schemata into a complex system through the process of organization. Schemata are developed through the process of adaptation.
This adaptation includes an equilibrium between the assimilation of

new information and accommodation of existing schemata to incorporate the new knowledge. Piaget further maintains that as these functionally invariant processes of organization and adaptation bring about a more complex, sophisticated cognitive system, the child will pass through a set sequence of stages of cognitive development. Infants are said to be in the sensorimotor stage, which is further divided into the following six substages:

Stage 1: Use of reflexes (birth to about 1 month)
Stage 2: Primary circular reactions (about 1 to 4 months)
Stage 3: Secondary circular reactions (about 4 to 8 months)
Stage 4: Coordination of secondary circular reactions (about 8 to 12 months)
Stage 5: Tertiary circular reactions (about 12 to 18 months)
Stage 6: Intervention of new means through mental combinations (about 18 to 24 months)

The attainment of the schema of the permanent object is the most significant aspect of the sensorimotor stage and is listed among other achievements by Baldwin. While Piaget's ideas have held up well under standardized testing, Bower has raised some question about the invariant stages that Piaget has proposed, particularly as they relate to conservation tasks.

Key terms in this section:

cognitive functioning	equilibrium
schemata	functional invariant
organization	stages of cognitive development
adaptation	sensorimotor stage
assimilation	schema of the permanent object
accommodation	conservation

Learning in Infancy

Learning is another important aspect of infant intelligence. Rather than depending solely on instincts, human infants display increasing effects of various forms of learning including habituation, imitation, classical conditioning, and instrumental (operant) conditioning. Pavlov's classical conditioning method of pairing conditioned stimuli (CS) with unconditioned stimuli (UCS) to elicit conditioned stimuli (CS) from unconditioned stimuli (UCS) has been attempted with both newborns and older infants. The operant conditioning technique of applying positive and negative reinforcers to alter or extinguish behavior has also been used. This is the basis of behavior modification therapy which stresses the use of contingent reward delivered on continuous or intermittent schedules to change behavior. Complex learning is also useful as it combines classical conditioning, which stresses a reactive child, with operant, which stresses an active child.

Key terms in this section:

learning
instinct
habituation
imitation
classical conditioning
conditioned stimulus (CS)
conditioned response (CR)
unconditioned stimulus (UCS)
unconditioned response (UCR)
instrumental (operant)
    conditioned

positive reinforcer
negative reinforcer
extinguishing
behavior modification
contingent (vs. noncontingent)
    reinforcement
continuous schedule of
    reinforcement
intermittent schedule of
    reinforcement
complex learning
reactive vs. active child

The Acquisition of Language

The development of skill in understanding and producing language
represents a major component of infant mental development. The
early prelinguistic speech of infants progresses through phases of
undifferentiated crying, differentiated crying, cooing, babbling,
lallation, echolalia, and expressive jargon. The development of
true linguistic speech also develops in stages including
holophrases, telegraphic speech, and grammatically correct utterances. Numerous factors have been identified which affect language
development; these include: mother-child interaction, maternal
education, social class, and practice. Several theories have been
developed to describe these factors and how they affect language.
Behaviorism stresses the effects of reinforcement of language.
Cultural relativism stresses the Worfian hypothesis. Interactionism stresses the role of cognitive development, and preformationism/
determinism stresses the role of innate mental abilities denoted
collectively as the language acquisition device (LAD).

Key terms in this section:

prelinguistic speech
undifferentiated crying
differentiated crying
cooing
babbling
lallation
echolalia
expressive jargon
linguistic speech

holophrase
telegraphic speech
behaviorism
cultural relativism
Worfian hypothesis
interactionism
preformationism/determinism
language acquisition device (LAD)

Measuring Infant Intelligence

It is difficult to measure intelligence in very young children and
infant scales do not predict well how a child will do on tests for
adults and older children. Lack of agreement on a definition of
intelligence contributes to the problem. Definitions have been

49

proposed by Terman, Piaget, Wechsler, Binet, Spearman, Thurston and Guilford. These various definitions have brought about a variety of measures of intelligence including the Intelligence Quotient (I.Q.), which compares mental age and chronological age, and the Developmental Quotient (D.Q.), which is used for infants. These measures are obtained by use of an intelligence test. The available tests vary in standardization sample, reliability and validity and in their emphasis on aptitude versus achievement. The list of infant intelligence tests includes the Gesell Developmental Schedules, the Cattell Infant Intelligence scale, the Bayley Scales, and the Brazelton Behavioral Assessment Scale.

Intelligence testing in infants is further complicated by the child's poor language skills, limited behavioral range and unknown motivation. In addition there are numerous environmental factors interacting with innate ability to affect test performance such as social class, family background, nutrition, child-rearing practices, level of stimulation and use of societal supports.

Key terms in this section:

intelligence quotient (IQ)	reliability
mental age	validity
chronological age	aptitude
developmental quotient (DQ)	achievement
standardization sample	

LEARNING OBJECTIVES

1. Describe the general principles that characterize Piaget's theory of cognitive development. (pp. 112-113)

2. Name the three major acquisitions of the sensorimotor stage as described by Baldwin. (p. 113)

   a.

   b.

c.

3. Trace the development of the schema of object permanence during the sensorimotor stage, and explain why it is important for infants to acquire this schema. (pp. 114-115)

4. List and briefly describe the six major substages of the sensorimotor stage of development. (pp. 114-115)

a.

b.

c.

d.

e.

f.

5. Discuss what research has indicated about Piaget's theory. (pp. 116-119)

6. Describe the position of Bower with regard to Piaget's stages of cognitive development. (pp. 117-119)

7. Describe the imitative abilities of young infants and briefly explain how these findings contradict Piaget's theory. (pp. 120-121)

8. Explain the difference between classical and operant conditioning. (pp. 121-124)

9. Describe past efforts to classically condition newborns and older infants. (pp. 122-123)

10. Describe past efforts to operantly condition newborns and older infants and briefly describe the application of these techniques in behavior modification. (pp. 123-125)

11. Trace the child's development of prelinguistic speech through seven phases. (pp. 127-128)

12. Describe the impact of each of the following on language development.

    a. Mother-child interaction (p. 129)

    b. Maternal education (pp. 129-130)

    c. Social class (p. 130)

    d. Practice (p. 130)

13. Briefly review the four major theories of language acquisition and explain how environmental/cultural theories differ from innate/maturational ones. (pp. 130-132)

14. Explain why it is difficult to assess infant intelligence. (pp. 136-137)

15. Review briefly the past definitions of intelligence. (pp. 132-134)

16. List and describe three major concerns in constructing intelligence tests. (pp. 134-136)

    a.

    b.

    c.

17. List and describe four major infant intelligence tests. (pp. 137-140)

    a.

b.

c.

d.

18. Discuss six major environmental influences on the intellectual
    development of the infant.   (pp. 141-147)

    a.

    b.

    c.

    d.

    e.

    f.

SELF TEST A

Circle the letter of the choice that completes each item.

1. According to Piaget, a child builds internal representations of the world called schemata and develops these into an integrated network through the process called: (a) assimilation; (b) accommodation; (c) organization; (d) equilibration.

2. The most important development during the sensorimotor stage is the development of: (a) goal-directed behavior; (b) the schema of the permanent object; (c) a relationship between objects and their sensory impressions; (d) conservation skills.

3. The last sensorimotor substage that does not include mental representations of external events is called: (a) secondary circular reactions stage; (b) coordination of secondary circular reactions stage; (c) tertiary circular reactions stage; (d) intervention of new means through mental combinations stage.

4. Two-year-old Jamie had a recent accident when her mother momentarily left her alone as she went to answer the phone and Jamie touched a hot stove. Now Jamie cries whenever the phone rings. Jamie's crying behavior is the result of: (a) habituation; (b) classical conditioning; (c) operant conditioning; (d) imitative learning.

5. Recent evidence suggests that classical conditioning of infants may not be possible until after the age of: (a) 1 year; (b) 6 months; (c) 1 month; (d) 1 week.

6. The stage of prelinguistic speech in which the child consciously imitates the sounds of others is called: (a) lallation; (b) cooing; (c) echolalia; (d) expressive jargon.

7. "Mommy go now." This is an example of: (a) echolalia; (b) expressive jargon; (c) telegraphic speech; (d) holophrastic speech.

8. Tests of infant intelligence: (a) are excellent predictors of later intelligence; (b) are heavily based on verbal abilities; (c) lack reliability; (d) stress sensory and motor skills.

9. A scale of infant intelligence which stresses the four main areas of motor behavior, adaptive behavior, language behavior, and personal-social behavior was devised by: (a) Bayley; (b) Gesell; (c) Cattell; (d) Brazelton.

10. Which of the following has not been shown to have a positive effect on infant intellectual development? (a) good nutrition; (b) having a mother who pushes for learning and is "overprotective"; (c) having a mother who serves mainly as a designer and consultant;

(d) being played with and actively interacted with at an early age.

PRACTICE EXERCISES

Completion

1. According to Piaget, the basic cognitive unit, called the

    schema, is created through adaptation, which is a two-

    step process involving both _acc_ and _ass_ .

2. Baldwin suggests that the three major developments of the

    sensorimotor period include: (a) relating _incoming sensory_ in-

    formation to _objects_ in the world; (b) recognizing the

    world as a _permanent_ place; and (c) developing

    goal-directed behavior.

3. In developing object permanence, during the _____

    _____ _____ substage of the sensorimotor stage
    a child will search for an object if part of it is showing but
    will fail to search if it is completely covered.

4. The awareness that matter does not change in quantity if it is

    rearranged is called _2nd conservation_ _conservation reaction_

5. _Learning_ is a change in behavior as a result of experience.

6. Moore and Meitzoff (1975) suggest that in the first few weeks

    of life babies can _imitate_ facial and hand gestures.
    Piaget maintained that this skill does not develop until around
    9 months of age.

7. The equation for classical conditioning is:

    Step 1   CS + _ucs_ → _ucr_

    Step 2   CS → _cr_

8. Research on classical conditioning indicates that such learning

    is possible for humans after _1_ month(s) of life.

9. Strings of sentence-like utterances which are made up of
    meaningless gibberish occur during the prelinguistic phase

    called ___expr___ ___jargon___ .

10. The ___Brazelton___ _____ scale
    assesses interactive behavior in infants, while the

    ___Cattel___ _____ _____ scale is a
    downward extension of the Stanford Binet test for 2- to 30-
    month-old infants.

Matching

In the blank to the left of each definition, write the letter that
indicates the term defined.

___d___ 1. The process of taking in new information

___f___ 2. The integration of schema into a single system

___a e___ 3. An active effort to reproduce something first achieved
           by chance

___g___ 4. Gradual decrease in responses to a constant stimulus

___i___ 5. The pairing of UCS and CS to bring about a conditioned
           response

___b___ 6. Providing contingent reinforcement for a response

___h___ 7. Early speech with one word used as an entire sentence

___j___ 8. Sentence composed only of words with high meaning

___c___ 9. Language one learns will shape a person's view of the
           world.

___e___ 10. Innate structures which make language development
            possible

a. primary circular reaction   f. organization
b. operant conditioning   g. habituation
c. Worfian hypothesis   h. holophrase
d. assimilation   i. classical conditioning
e. language acquisition device j. telegraphic speech

SELF TEST B

Circle the letter of the choice that completes each item.

1. The process of changing existing schema to adjust to new information is called: (a) organization; (b) adaptation; (c) assimilation; (d) accommodation.

58

2. Bower suggests that Piaget is incorrect in his description of children's understanding of: (a) object permanence; (b) conservation; (c) imitation; (d) language.

3. Which of the following is proposed by Baldwin as a major sensorimotor development? (a) separation of objects and their sensory impressions; (b) development of conservation skill; (c) development of goal-directed behavior; (d) all of these.

4. A response will occur more consistently if it is reinforced: (a) intermittently; (b) continuously; (c) aversively; (d) never.

5. Language which includes short sentences with only high-content words is called: (a) echolalia; (b) expressive jargon; (c) telegraphic; (d) holophrastic.

6. Middle-class mothers talked more to their babies than did working class mothers because they had: (a) different beliefs about infants; (b) more time; (c) higher verbal skills; (d) fewer children.

7. The cultural relativist's view of language stresses: (a) reinforcement (b) innate structures; (c) cognitive development; (d) social necessity.

8. A test which measures what it is supposed to measure has: (a) generalizability; (b) standardization; (c) reliability; (d) validity.

9. The Gesell Developmental Schedules cover four major areas. These are motor, social, adaptive and: (a) language behavior; (b) personality adjustment; (c) parent-child interaction; (d) visual-spatial reasoning.

10. Which of the following has not been shown to affect the intellect l development of infants? (a) nutrition; (b) heredity; (c) parental divorce; (d) use of societal supports.

VIGNETTES

1. You are babysitting for 12-month-old Angela, and to keep her amused you are rolling a ball back and forth between the two of you. On one occasion, the ball rolls under a nearby chair. Angela watches it and immediately goes under the chair and retrieves it. On the very next roll, it goes under the chair but comes out again, in full view with Angela watching, and goes behind the couch. Angela immediately does under the chair to get the ball, can't find it and begins to wail at the top of her lungs. At this moment, Angela's mother returns and asks, "What's wrong with my Angela? Why is she crying?" How would you explain?

2.   Mr. and Mrs. Daley have a 3-year-old son, Eric, who constantly engages in temper tantrums to get his way. This behavior is particularly problematic at the preschool he attends. In fact, unless this behavior is brought under control, Eric will have to be taken out of school, because he disrupts the entire program. Desperate, Mr. and Mrs. Daley have tried to completely ignore Eric's tantrums and have been able to do so on several occasions. Often, however, he gets so violent that Mr. and Mrs. Daley "just have to give in." Mr. and Mrs. Daley have come to you for help. What are they doing wrong? What would you suggest?

3.   Friends have just told you that their infant brother is being tested by a psychologist. The infant is 24 months old, and your friends claim that the reason for the test is that the child is "gifted" and the parents want to determine how well the child is likely to do in school, college, and so on. How would you respond?

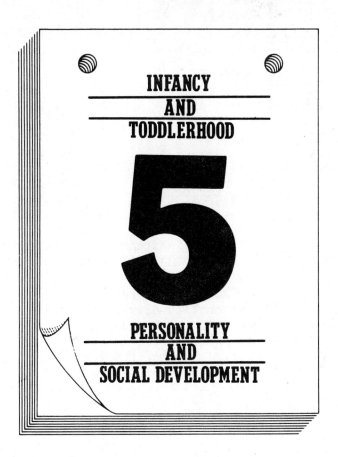

INFANCY
AND
TODDLERHOOD

5

PERSONALITY
AND
SOCIAL DEVELOPMENT

INTEGRATOR

We have seen that the infancy period is one marked by astounding physical and intellectual growth. Beginning with the simple reflex behaviors and immature sensory skills described in Chapter 3, the infant begins to learn and think about the world as described in Chapter 4. People make up a crucial component of that world, however, and Chapter 5 will consider the infant's development of the social skills necessary for interaction with others. Much of how people act toward the child will reflect the child's own personal, unique way of viewing and behaving toward others. Thus personality, social interaction, physical development, and intellectual functioning are all interwoven and continue to be mutually interactive throughout the life span. The theories of Freud and Erikson, introduced in Chapter 5, will therefore be discussed again in later chapters covering personality development and function at later life-span periods. The role of family and friends will be a reoccurring theme as we continue to trace the development of the person through childhood, adolescence, parenthood, and grandparenthood.

OVERVIEW

What Emotions Do Babies Have?

The expression of emotions is a major component of personality development. However, the study of emotions in infants is very difficult. It is difficult to determine what babies feel by watching what they do. Several guesses about what emotions a baby feels vary from Watson's love, rage, and fear to Bridge's undifferentiated excitement. Today the emphasis is on interrelationships between expressions of feeling, measures, timing, contexts, and individual differences of emotional response.

Crying is an obvious infant behavior that seems related to emotions. Wolff describes four types of crying: (1) rhythmical crying, (2) angry crying, (3) pain crying, and (4) cry of frustration. Prompt responding to a baby's crying by the caretaker is thought to be beneficial for positive personality development. Smiling, a basic means of communication for infants, appears early and gradually increases in social significance during the first three to four months. At 4 months of age, laughing in infants emerges, signaling an important cognitive advancement.

Key terms in this section:

undifferentiated excitement	pain crying
rhythmic crying	cry of frustration
angry crying	

Personality Development in Infants

This section describes the personality theories of Sigmund Freud and Erik Erikson. Freud thought that humans go through several stages of psychosexual development during a period of primary narcissism. During this period, children cathect to various sources of gratification with a different source denoting each stage. In infancy, these stages are the oral and anal stages. Experiences during these stages determine adult adjustment patterns and personality traits such as an oral personality or an anal personality.

In contrast to Freud's stress on biological determinants of personality, Erikson focused on societal influences. According to this theory, ego growth is determined by the way the person resolves certain basic "crises." In infancy, these crises are basic trust vs. basic mistrust, which rests upon the quality of the mother-infant relationship, and autonomy vs. shame and doubt, which rests on parent child-rearing practices and maturational pressures.

Key terms in this section:

primary narcissism	sources of gratification
cathect	oral stage

```
anal stage                          autonomy vs. shame/doubt
oral personality                    quality vs. quantity of mother-
anal personality                        infant relationship
basic trust vs. mistrust
```

The Infant in the Family

Recent changes have occurred in psychologists' way of viewing the
impact of the family on infant development. Psychologists have
assumed that all children are raised in a nuclear family. This
view has focused on only the mother's impact. The focus has now
broadened to include consideration of the impact of fathers, siblings, child-rearing practices, "nontraditional" settings, and the
child's own behavior. It has been shown, for example, that
parents react to children based on the child's temperament. Such
findings have led to identification of three broad classes of
temperamental types of children: (1) the easy child, (2) the
difficult child, and (3) the slow-to-warm-up child. Temperament
can be a crucial factor for parents to consider in making decisions
on demand vs. structured feeding schedules and general rearing
practices.

Family constellation is another recent innovation in the approach
to family impact on infant development. The impact of being an
only child and of sibling influences are major research interests.

Sex differences is a very popular, recent issue for all periods of
life-span development, and infancy is not an exception. From conception on, there are clear anatomical and physical differences
between males and females. Physical vulnerability of males has
been well documented, while other purported sex differences in infants have had equivocal support. What sex differences may exist
may be related to sex differences in parent-infant interaction.
Sex-role stereotyping, especially by fathers, is prevalent from
birth on.

Key terms in this section:

```
temperament                         the slow-to-warm-up child
the easy child                      family constellation
the difficult child                 sex-role stereotypes
```

The Family's Role in Personality Development

The mother's role in the personality development of the child has
received considerable theoretical and empirical attention in the
past. Interest has recently expanded to include the father's impact as well. Continued efforts to consider the entire family are
called for.

Studies with animals have shown the importance of imprinting and
contact comfort provided by surrogate mothers in forming parent-

offspring bonds. One cannot, however, extrapolate these findings directly to humans, because it seems clear that maternal love is not an instinct.

Attachment is an active, affectionate, reciprocal relationship specifically between two individuals as distinguished from all other persons. Mother-child attachment may be related to the quality of care she provides, the mother's personality, and experiences centering around parenthood, especially in the hospital right after delivery. The infant's contribution is also important, and its behavior reflects four overlapping stages of attachment behavior. Studies on cuddlers vs. noncuddlers and daughter/son attachment indicate that the baby's personality and sex may also affect the strength of attachments.

Stranger anxiety is a common, but not universal, development in infancy. Numerous theories have been offered to explain why some children develop a fear of strangers while others do not.

Studies of maternal deprivation of institutionalized infants can lead to hospitalism and point to the need for consistent mothering in a stimulating environment. Enriching the environment of institutionalized infants has resulted in significant emotional and intellectual gains for these children. Separation from parents due to hospitalization results in a separation-anxiety response which progresses through stages of protest, despair and detachment.

For short-term, temporary separations, numerous factors can contribute to the ease of separation. It is clear that not only is the fact of separation important but also the reason behind it.

The father's attachment to the infant, or engrossment, has only recently become the subject of research. While studies have indicated that this relationship may be more important to the infant's development than previously thought, questions remain concerning the factors which affect engrossment and the consequences of father absence and attachment.

Key terms in this section:

imprinting	hospitalism vs. hospitalization
surrogate mother	separation anxiety
attachment	protest stage
cuddlers vs. noncuddlers	despair stage
stranger anxiety	detachment stage
maternal deprivation	engrossment

Friendship in Infancy

The study of friendship falls into the realm of social cognition, which uses sociometry to investigate friendship and its development.

In infancy, recent data point to early patterns of friendship behavior and wide individual differences in sociability. The development of friendships early on seems to follow an orderly developmental pattern from a first stage of object-centered contacts to
a second stage of trying to get responses from another to a third
role-switching stage. Opportunity to develop infant friendships
is a major ingredient in its development.

Key terms in this section:

social cognition	try-to-get-others-to-respond
sociometry	stage
object-centered stage	role-switching stage

LEARNING OBJECTIVES

1. Explain briefly why it is difficult to answer the question,
   "What emotions do babies have?" and describe early attempts
   to describe infant emotions by Watson and Bridges. (pp. 152-
   153)

2. Name and differentiate among the four patterns of infant cries
   described by Wolff. (p. 155)

   a.

   b.

   c.

   d.

3. Describe the social functions that are served by infant smiling and laughter. (pp. 155-156)

4. Describe the oral and anal stages of development and the adult behavior patterns that result from being fixated at each of these stages. (p. 158)

5. Explain Erikson's notion of psychosocial crises and give examples of satisfactory and unsatisfactory resolutions of crises I and II. (pp. 158-159)

6. Describe the factors that are cited as contributing to the successful resolution of crises I and II in Erikson's theory. (p. 159)

   a. Trust vs. mistrust

   b. Autonomy vs. shame and doubt

7. Review the evidence that children vary in temperament beginning with birth and tell why this concept is of such practical importance to parents. (pp. 160-162)

8. Describe the possible effects of being an only child. (p. 163)

9. Give two possible explanations for the fact that males are more vulnerable than females to life stresses. (pp. 163-164)

10. Describe the differences in the ways that parents treat their male and female children. (pp. 164-165)

11. Explain the role of imprinting in the mother-child inter- actions of various species. (pp. 166-167)

12. Describe the differences the Harlows found between infant rhesus monkeys raised with wire as opposed to cloth mother surrogates. (p. 167)

13. List the factors that seem to be important in awakening mother love. (pp. 167-169)

14. Describe the four overlapping stages of attachment noted by Ainsworth in African babies. (p. 169)

    a.

    b.

    c.

    d.

15. Briefly describe how a baby's gender and personality can affect attachment. (p. 170)

16. Explain the significance of stranger anxiety. (pp. 170-172)

17. Describe the conditions which lead to hospitalism and actions that can be taken to lessen the effects of institutionalization. (pp. 173-174)

18. Briefly list and describe the three stages of separation anxiety as defined by Bowlby. (pp. 174-175)

19. Explain the term engrossment as used to describe the father's attachment to his child. (pp. 176-178)

20. Describe factors which contribute to sociability in infancy. (pp. 179-181)

SELF TEST A

Circle the letter of the choice that completes each item.

1. John B. Watson claimed that infants are born with three major
emotions: (a) love, jealousy, and fear; (b) love, rage, and fear;
(c) love, fear, and undifferentiated excitement; (d) none of these;
Watson thought all emotions are learned.

2. John, a 3-week-old infant, is crying. His cry is distinguished
by a sudden onset, is very loud, and was not preceded by moaning.
John is exhibiting a(n): (a) anger cry; (b) pain cry; (c) rhythmical cry; (d) cry of frustration.

3. Smiling is an important behavior in infants because it: (a) is
a powerful social stimulus; (b) represents important cognitive
development; (c) relieves the infant's distress more effectively
than crying; (d) is a clear sign of joy in infancy as early as the
first week.

4. During the period of primary narcissism, children operate on
the _____ principle. (a) wholistic; (b) reality; (c) pleasure;
(d) autonomy.

5. A baby sleeps deeply, eats well, enjoys bowel relaxation, and
generally feels that the world is a good place in which to live.
According to Erikson, he is showing: (a) basic trust; (b) autonomy;
(c) anal cathexis; (d) oral gratification.

6. Lucy is a quiet infant who is mild in her responses, both
positive and negative. She shows a distinct dislike for new situations but eventually she gets used to and enjoys new things.
Thomas and Chess would identify Lucy as a(n): (a) difficult child;
(b) easy child; (c) withdrawn child; (d) slow-to-warm-up child.

7. Which of the following is true of early behavioral differences
between the sexes? (a) Mothers talk to daughters more than sons.
(b) Mothers are more indulgent and warmer toward baby sons than
daughters. (c) Fathers treat sons more gently than daughters.
(d) Parents tend to treat sons and daughters about the same for the
first 4-6 weeks.

8. The tendency of newly hatched chicks to follow the first object
they see is called: (a) cathexis; (b) love; (c) imprinting; (d)
attachment.

9. Kip, a 12-month-old, is in the hospital. Kip accepts care from
a succession of nurses, is willing to eat and be sociable, but is
apathetic when his mother visits. According to Bowlby, Kip is
showing the _____ stage of separation anxiety. (a) protest;
(b) despair; (c) detachment; (d) adjusted.

10. "Engrossment" refers to a(n): (a) father's intense attachment to his baby; (b) baby's fascination with his feet; (c) amotivational state; (d) extreme level of maternal attachment.

PRACTICE EXERCISES

Completion

Supply the words or phrases that best complete these sentences.

1. In 1919, John B. Watson, the behaviorist, claimed that infants

   are born with three major emotions: _love_, _rage_,

   and _fear_.

2. Wolff (1969) found different patterns between infants' basic rhythmical cries and their cries of anger, pain, and frustra--

   tion: the _basic_ _rhythmic_ cry (often called the "hunger

   cry," but not always associated with hunger); the _anger_
   cry (a variation of the basic cry in which a baby forces

   excess air through the vocal cords); the _pain_ cry (distinguished by a sudden onset of loud crying, without preliminary moaning, and an initial long cry followed by an extended

   period of breath-holding): and the cry of _frustration_
   (starting from silence with no long breath-holding, and with
   the first two or three cries long and drawn out).

3. Children's greatest pleasure during the _anal_ stage comes from moving their bowels.

4. According to Erikson, the bond between mother and infant is an important determinant of an infant's sense of trust, with

   the _qual_ of the mother-child tie being more important

   than its _quant_.

5. Most developmental theories and projects have been based on

   the premise that children grow up in a _nuclear_ family and

   that the _mother_ assumes primary care of the child. Thus,

   the emphasis has been on the _mother_ - _child_ bond.

71

6. The infant's basic behavioral style that appears to be inborn is called _temperament_.

7. If you were your parents' ___1st___ child, you may be more likely to want company in times of stress, to be enrolled in a college, and to make it into Who's Who.

8. ___Attachment___ is an active, affectionate, reciprocal relationship specifically between two individuals, as distinguished from all other persons.

9. The devastating effect of institutionalizing healthy children for long periods of time is called _hospitalism_.

10. Bowlby (1960) found that hospitalized 15- to 30-month-old infants went through three fairly well-defined stages of ___separation___ ___anxiety___. In the ___protest___ stage, infants actively try to get their mother back by crying, shaking the crib, and throwing themselves about; in the ___despair___ stage, infants diminish active movements, cry monotonously or intermittently, and become withdrawn and inactive; in the ___detachment___ stage, children accept care from a succession of nurses and are willing to eat, play with toys, smile, and be sociable.

True-False

Circle T if the statement is true, F if the statement is false.

T (F) 1. Emotions are easily assessed in infancy because even from birth humans exhibit clear emotional responses.

(T) F 2. Pain cries have sudden onset, no preliminary moaning, and involve a long initial cry followed by breath-holding.

(T) F 3. Anal adult personality can be described as involving obsessive preciseness, rigidity, and pedantry.

T (F) 4. The "terrible two's" represent a child's struggle with what Erikson calls the basic trust-mistrust crisis.

(T) F 5. It has been found that a child's temperament is an important factor for parents to consider in raising their children.

(T) F 6. Only children have been shown to suffer both intel-

72

lectually and socially from being their parents' only
offspring.

(T) F 7. Recent reports show that parents, particularly fathers,
persist in employing sex-role stereotypes when dealing
with their children.

T (F) 8. Data on imprinting clearly show that all forms of
mother-child bonding are genetically controlled instincts.

(T) F 9. A mother's personality and the opportunity to interact
as much as possible with her infant in the hospital have
both been shown to greatly affect attachment.

(T) F 10. Data indicate that the amount of time parents spend
with their infant is the major factor affecting strength
of attachment and engrossment.

Word Scramble

Unscramble the ten items. Then arrange the circled letters to
complete the sentence below.

1. _R_ _H_ _Y_ _I_ _H_ _M_ (O) _C_ _ _
    I   M   R   Y   C   H   T   H
   Crying associated with hunger

2. _C_ _A_ _J_ _h_ _E_ _C_ (T)
    C   E   C   H   A   T   T
   Form attachment to source of gratification

3. _0_ _R_ (A) _L_
    L   A   0   R
   First psychosexual stage

4. _1_ _m_ (P) _R_ _L_ (M) _I_ _L_ _N_ _b_
    P   N   I   N   G   I   M   R   T   I
   Instinctual attachment in ducks

5. _A_ _I_ _T_ _A_ _C_ _H_ _m_ (E) _N_ _I_
    T   E   H   A   C   T   N   A   T   M
   Active, affectionate, reciprocal relationship

6. _S_ _T_ _R_ _A_ _N_ _b_ (E) _R_
    T   R   E   S   G   N   R   A
   Anxiety associated with unfamiliar people

73

7. A O S I _ _ _ _ _ _ O
   P H S A O T I L M S I
   Deterioration with prolonged institutionalization

8. R P O I E S L
   O P E T T R S
   First stage of separation anxiety

9. E N G K O S Y M E N T
   S G E M T E N N R O S
   Strong father-infant relationship

10. S O G R A L _ O _ _
   C O S M E I Y O R T
   Used to study infant sociability

Slow-to-warm-up and easy are two types of infants'

T E M P E R A M E N T.

SELF TEST B

Circle the letter of the choice that completes each item.

1. According to Wolff, the variation to the basic cry in which an infant forces excess air through the vocal cords is: (a) angry cry; (b) pain cry; (c) frustration cry; (d) rhythmic cry.

2. Laughing is an important emotional response because: (a) It is more obvious and therefore easier to study than smiling. (b) It is the first true emotional response to develop. (c) It denotes cognitive awareness of incongruity. (d) It is an audible response which parents can detect and respond to without actually seeing the infant.

3. Erikson would define "shame" as: (a) loss of hope; (b) rage turned against the self; (c) precocious conscience; (d) maternal cathectus.

4. Nancy's parents wish to use a demand-feeding schedule. That is, they will let Nancy decide when she is hungry and when she should eat. They will have the greatest success if Nancy's temperament places her in the: (a) slow-to-warm-up class; (b) difficult-child class; (c) easy-child class; (d) nonrhythmic class.

5. Which of the following is not true of sex differences in

infancy? (a) Males develop more rapidly. (b) Females are more likely to survive. (c) More males than females are conceived. (d) At birth, males tend to be heavier than females.

6. "Temperament" means: (a) the basic behavioral style of an infant; (b) the home "atmosphere" of environment; (c) tendency toward anger or rage; (d) tendency to react to frustration.

7. Bobby wants company in times of stress, is in Who's Who, and went to an elite college. Most likely, Bobby: (a) comes from a large family; (b) is a first-born child; (c) has an older sister; (d) is an identical twin.

8. Harlow's studies with rhesus monkeys showed the babies preferred the surrogate "mother" that: (a) fed them; (b) was warm; (c) was covered with soft cloth; (d) moved.

9. According to Ainsworth, a 2-month-old infant would most likely: (a) not respond to people or things around him; (b) show a sharp defined attachment to the mother; (c) cry, smile, and babble more to the mother; (d) respond indiscriminately to anyone.

10. Enriching the environment of maternally deprived children: (a) has little, if any, effect; (b) is effective only if performed by trained professionals; (c) seems to have a positive long-term effect; (d) causes hospitalism.

VIGNETTES

1. The text points out the interactive nature of children's smiles and vocalizations as well as those of adults. What special problems might you need to address if you were developing a training program in effective parenting for blind or deaf parents.

2. A physician has come to you looking for advice on a recently hospitalized patient. The patient is a 2½-year-old male who has chronic hypertension. The child is not responding favorably to hospitalization. He is very aggressive and cries frequently. He seems to be afraid of everyone. What would you suggest to help calm the child?

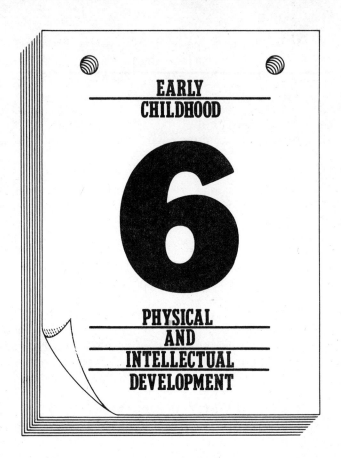

EARLY
CHILDHOOD

6

PHYSICAL
AND
INTELLECTUAL
DEVELOPMENT

INTEGRATOR

This chapter continues the description of physical and mental growth
begun in Chapters 3 and 4 but proceeds from infancy into the early
school years. The important interactions among physical, mental,
and personality development will again be emphasized. Chapter 7
will provide a more detailed account of some of the aspects of
personality development that are introduced in this chapter.
Piaget's concepts will be a central focus as we consider cognitive
growth beyond the infancy stage of sensorimotor reasoning and examine the skills of young children.

OVERVIEW

Physical Growth and Motor Development

The first topic considered is physical and motor development. During early childhood, growth slows to a steady 2 to 3 inches per
year while nervous, muscular, and skeletal systems are maturing.
Dental disorders represent a major concern during this period.
Cavity rates and other dental problems are affected by nutrition,
thumb sucking, and ethnic background. Most children grow normally
during these years; however, abnormal growth can result from

malfunctions in the pituitary gland leading to idiopathic hypopituitarism, from emotional conditions, or from unknown causes as
in failure-to-thrive infants.

Motor development during the early childhood years is rapid and is
marked with large gains in eye-hand and small-muscle coordination.
In general, boys excel in strength tasks, while girls are superior
in small-muscle coordination. Table 6-2 outlines the motor skills
of 3-, 4-, and 5-year-olds.

Key terms in this section:

pituitary gland   failure-to-thrive syndrome
idiopathic hypopituitarism

Abused and Neglected Children

The next section describes a serious problem in our country--that
of child abuse and neglect. It is estimated that "battered child
syndrome" affects 360 children out of a million, and abusing
parents come from all socioeconomic levels. However, most abusing
parents tend to come from lower socioeconomic levels and have suffered abuse and emotional deprivation in their own childhood.
Children who have been abused act very distrustful of others, which
may result from or contribute to the child abuse syndrome. Our
high rate of child abuse may be due in part to our acceptance of
physical force in child rearing. Generally speaking, family therapy
is the treatment of choice in cases of child abuse or neglect.

Key term in this section:

Battered child syndrome

Piaget's Preoperational Stage (2 to 7 Years)

At about age 2, children enter what Piaget calls the preoperational
stage. This stage ushers in symbolic function, making it possible
for children to use signifiers, such as symbols and signs, to represent significates.

The exhibition of deferred imitation, symbolic play, and language
are interpreted as evidence for the development of symbolic function
by the preoperational child. The thought of the preoperational
child is further characterized by egocentrism (inability to take
the role of another person), centration (focusing on one aspect of
a situation to the neglect of others), and irreversibility (not
understanding that an operation can go both ways). Understanding
the nature of preoperational thought has widespread practical ap-
plications in areas dealing with children.

The acquisition of specific cognitive abilities such as seriation
and classification has been a major focus for Piagetian researchers.

In classification, for example, it has been learned that young children produce figural collections until age 4½ to 6 or 7 when quasi-classifications are produced. By age 7 or 8 children can classify correctly. Although there is some evidence that these abilities may be accelerated through specific training, the ultimate value of such programs is a matter of debate.

Key terms in this section:

preoperational stage	language
symbolic function	egocentrism
signifiers	centration
significates	irreversibility
symbols	seriation
signs	classification
deferred imitation	figural collection
symbolic play	quasi-classifications

School in Early Childhood

Preschools and day-care centers have recently experienced a tremendous surge in popularity. The programs in such centers vary greatly and encompass profit and nonprofit, use of certified and untrained teachers, emphasis on cognitive and affective development, and so on. The primary value of such schools seems to be that they provide a wide variety of intellectual and social experiences which prepare the child for later social and school experiences and make school seem fun.

Preschools vary in their orientation and methods of teaching. The Montessori method is based on a prepared environment and stresses motor, sensory, and language education through a child-centered format. Preschools for deprived children, including Operation Head Start, Home Start, and the Brookline Early Education Project, stress preparation for learning. Such programs have had beneficial, if sometimes short-lived, effects on deprived children.

Day-care centers also vary and fall into three general categories: comprehensive child development programs, developmental day care, and custodial child care. The experiences gained in each type of center ranges from excellent to mediocre. Staff training in child-related fields, type of funding, and child/staff ratio have been cited as important factors in determining level of benefit gained by the child. Data are presently insufficient for drawing conclusions about the benefits or harm of day care in general.

Finally, many children attend kindergarten, an experience that bridges nursery school and the structure of more formal schooling. Children who attend kindergarten generally do better in reading activities later on.

Key terms in this section:

Montessori method
prepared environment
motor education
sensory education
language education
child-centered format

Operation Head Start
Home Start
Brookline Early Education Project
comprehensive child development
    programs
developmental day care
custodial day care

Language in Early Childhood

From age 3 to age 7, children's language grows in complexity and
sophistication at a phenomenal rate. The early language behavior
of children is of two main types, egocentric and socialized. Egocentric speech fails to take into account the listener's needs and
may be used as an entertaining activity, wish fulfillment as in
monologue, or to achieve control over behavior as in collective
monologue. Social speech is intended communication. Such language
is evident early on but continues to develop throughout the early
childhood period.

How children learn language is a fascinating question. Language
acquisition is probably not learned through simple imitation of or
reinforcement by adults. Yet interaction with adults is important.
When this interaction is diminished--for whatever reason--language
skills take longer to develop. Such is the case for twins who must
share adult attention.

Social class is another variable affecting development. Sociolinguistics is a discipline which attempts to determine what causes
the different language patterns often associated with a deprived,
low socioeconomic background. Bernstein, for example, postulates
that the use of restricted codes among lower-social-class language
users contributes to language patterns not found among middle-class
users who employ elaborated codes. Attempts to improve the compatibility of the language skills of lower-class children to
"typical English language" have included family intervention and
working directly with the children.

Key terms in this section:

egocentric language
monologue
collective monologue
socialized language

language acquisition
sociolinguistics
restricted codes
elaborated codes

Intelligence in Young Children: Its Measurement and Development

The meaning of intelligence as a way of predicting potential is
first of value during the preschool years when tests can include
verbal items. Popular tests include the Stanford-Binet and the

Wechsler Preschool and Primary Scale of Intelligence (WPPSI).

How well a child scores on an "intelligence test" is determined by a number of variables. Emotional and social functioning, temperament, parental child-rearing practices, socioeconomic status, and viewing specialized television programs have all been identified as variables that can enhance intelligence-test performance.

Key terms in this section:

Stanford-Binet test
Wechsler Preschool and Primary
    Scale of Intelligence test

LEARNING OBJECTIVES

1. Describe the general course of physical growth during early childhood. (p. 188)

2. Discuss the factors that are related to dental problems in early childhood. (p. 188)

3. Describe the current recommendation of experts concerning thumb sucking by toddlers. (p. 188)

4. Describe the following three factors that may be responsible for abnormal physical growth. (p. 189)

Pituitary malfunction

Emotional factors

Failure to thrive

5. Describe the general features of motor development of both girls and boys during early childhood. (pp. 189-192)

6. Describe the behavior that is typical of an abused child but that is not found in his or her nonabused sibling. (pp. 193-194)

7. Discuss the factors that may be responsible for the occurrence of child abuse. (p. 194)

8. Describe the methods that are used to help abused children and their families. (p. 195)

9. The preoperational stage ushers in the symbolic function, during which children demonstrate deferred imitation, symbolic play, and language. Define each of these terms. (p. 196)

   Symbolic function

   Deferred imitation

   Symbolic play

   Language

10. Differentiate among the terms "signifier," "significate," "symbol," and "sign." (p. 196)

11. Define and give an example of the following characteristics of preoperational thought. (pp. 196-197)

    Egocentrism

Irreversibility

Centration

12. Explain with examples the following cognitive concepts of preschool children. (pp. 198-199)

Seriation

Classification

13. Briefly describe the evidence that shows that Piagetian concepts can be accelerated, and comment on the utility of such a practice. (p. 199)

14. List the possible advantages to a child who attends a preschool. (pp. 200-201)

15. List and describe the three major facets of the Montessori method. (pp. 201-202)

a.

b.

c.

16. Briefly describe the following compensatory education programs. (p. 203)

    Operation Head Start

    Home Start

    Brookline Early Education Project

17. List and describe the three types of child care defined by the Department of Health, Education, and Welfare. (pp. 203-204)

    a.

    b.

c.

18. Describe the type of day care in which children do best ac-
    cording to the 1978 Abt Associates study. (p. 204)

19. Tell what is known about the effects of day care on children.
    (pp. 204-205)

20. Describe the typical speech of the following age periods.
    (p. 206)

    a. Age 3-4

    b. Age 4-5

    c. Age 5-6

21. Differentiate between egocentric and socialized speech. (pp. 206-
    207)

22. Review research evidence that socialized speech begins early in childhood. (p

23. Tell what parents might do to enhance the learning of language by their children.

24. Describe six variables that have been shown to affect performance on intelligence tests.

SELF TEST A

Circle the letter of the choice that completes each item.

1. Physical development during the preschool years: (a) may be strongly influenced by poor nutrition; (b) is not affected by emotional factors; (c) is more rapid than during infancy; (d) is identical for males and females.

2. Dental cavities have recently been found to be more frequent among: (a) poor children; (b) children from higher-income families; (c) black children; (d) children who suck their thumb after age 2.

3. The gland that secretes the hormone that controls normal growth

is the: (a) adrenal; (b) pituitary; (c) idiopathic; (d) hypothalamus.

4. Which of the following is <u>not</u> true of child abuse? (a) Most victims are under the age of 3. (b) Abusing parents may pick one child as a scapegoat. (c) Child abuse is a major problem in all cultures. (d) Child abuse is found only in low socioeconomic groups.

5. Samson is playing on the floor. He takes a small rectangular block and pushes it along while making a sound like an automobile engine. He pushes his block down a play road he has built with strips of paper. Samson is exhibiting: (a) sign manipulation; (b) deferred imitation; (c) symbolic language; (d) symbolic play.

6. Joann walks into the room and announces to her parents that she has drawn a picture of her family. She asks her parents to look at it but holds it up so that only she can see the picture. Her parents can only see the back of the paper, and when they ask to see it Joann just holds the picture closer to herself but doesn't turn it around. Joann's behavior is due to: (a) egocentrism; (b) centration; (c) irreversibility; (d) symbolic function.

7. Studies of preschool programs for deprived children: (a) show no real effects; (b) indicate a need to begin programs earlier in the child's development; (c) are most effective when the child is 5 or 6 years of age; (d) do more harm than good.

8. _____ speech is considered noncommunicative by Piaget. (a) Egocentric; (b) Social; (c) Collective; (d) Personalized.

9. Middle-class mothers were found by Bernstein to use: (a) elaborated speech codes; (b) restricted speech codes; (c) sociolinguistic speech codes; (d) short controlling commands.

10. Which of the following has <u>not</u> been shown to be beneficial to intellectual achievement: (a) parental warmth; (b) curious, involved mothers; (c) parental acceleration; (d) high socioeconomic standing.

PRACTICE EXERCISES

Completion

Supply the words or phrases that best complete these sentences.

1. During the preschool years, physical growth occurs at the

rate of __2__ to __3__ inches per year. In general, girls are slightly _smaller_ and _lighter_ than boys at this age.

2. Children who are abnormally small for no apparent reason are often called _failure_-_to_-_thrive_ children.

3. The greatest killer of infants 6 to 12 months old is _physical_ _abuse_. After 1 year, it is second only to _accident_.

4. Our society's high rate of child abuse may be partly an outgrowth of our general acceptance of _physical_ _force_ in child rearing.

5. Traditional _psychotherapy_ is often ineffective in dealing with the battered-child syndrome. However, the use of _mother_ _surrogates_, who help with everyday problems, has been found to be effective.

6. According to Piaget, words and numerals are _signs_, whereas more personal representations are _symbols_.

7. _Deferred_ _imitation_ explains the mechanism whereby children see something, form a mental representation of it, and later imitate the activity.

8. Between 2 and 4 years of age, children do not sort out shapes but rather they make _figural_ collections.

9. O'Connor (1975) compared 3½- and 5-year-olds from two different nursery schools. The _age_-_grading_ made no difference in the children's behaviors, but the _adult_-_child_ ratio did have some effect. In the school with the _____ (higher/lower) adult-child ratio, children interacted more with adults and less with other children.

10. The Office of Child Development has identified three types of child care: _____ child development programs, _____ _____ _____, and

88

_____ _____ _____.

Matching

In the blank to the left of each definition, write the letter that indicates the term defined.

_o_ 1. hormonally based abnormal growth

_i_ 2. publicly shared signifier

_n_ 3. things represented symbolically

_m_ 4. focusing on only one aspect of a situation

_e_ 5. arranging stimuli according to at least one dimension

_f_ 6. carefully planned arrangement of preschool surroundings

_h_ 7. early-education program for deprived children

_k_ 8. early-education program for 3-year-olds and younger

_a_ 9. child care providing only physical safety

_b_ 10. most beneficial type of child care for disadvantaged

_c_ 11. talking to oneself

_d_ 12. talking to another child

_l_ 13. speech for communication

_j_ 14. language code of low socioeconomic groups

_g_ 15. television program that enhances preschoolers' intelligence test performance

a. custodial
b. comprehensive development
c. monologue
d. collective monologue
e. seriation
f. prepared environment
g. "Sesame Street"
h. Operation Head Start
i. sign
j. restricted
k. Brookline Early Education Project
l. socialized
m. centration
n. significates
o. idiopathic hypopituitarism

SELF TEST B

1. When growth retardation is caused by hormonal deficiency: (a) there is no known treatment; (b) a proper diet can be used as treatment; (c) injections of human growth hormone can increase the rate of growth; (d) psychological counseling to solve family conflict is needed.

2. As contrasted to girls (during the preschool years), boys:

(a) show better small-muscle coordination; (b) are better able to hop and skip; (c) are stronger and have more muscle; (d) show superior limb coordination.

3. The "failure-to-thrive" syndrome is caused by: (a) a poor diet; (b) a hormone deficiency; (c) factors which are not clearly understood at this time; (d) emotional upset.

4. Which of the following is not true of child abuse? (a) Usually, both parents inflict injuries. (b) Reported abuse comes most often in large, poor families. (c) Child abuse is rare in cultures with strong taboos against striking children. (d) Parents who abuse their children are often abused themselves when small.

5. One of the more effective ways of helping abusive parents is: (a) traditional psychotherapy; (b) leaving them alone to solve their own problems; (c) the use of "mother surrogates"; (d) pressing criminal assault charges.

6. Jimmy is asked to "put the things that belong together in a box" and is then shown a multitude of different colored geometric shapes. Jimmy responds by randomly choosing seven shapes of varying color, and using these to make a design in the box Jimmy has produced a: (a) true class; (b) figural collection; (c) quasi-class; (d) symbolic group.

7. Bernice lives in a poor ghetto area. When she speaks to her children she uses short commands such as "Shut up!," "No!," and "Inna minute." These are examples of: (a) telegraphic speech; (b) elaborated language codes; (c) restricted language codes; (d) egocentric speech.

8. Which of the following is not an area of emphasis in Montessori-type preschools? (a) sensory education; (b) motor education; (c) language education; (d) prosocial education.

9. A program for deprived children which went into the family environment to provide early education was called: (a) Home Start; (b) Operation Head Start; (c) Brookline Early Education Project; (d) Homelife Intervention.

10. Which of the following has been shown to improve preschoolers' performances on intelligence tests? (a) pushing parents; (b) quite retiring temperament; (c) warm nurturing parents; (d) rigid parent who enforces the rules.

VIGNETTES

1. Many parents become very concerned about thumb sucking by their children. If asked whether this behavior is indicative of "emotiona

problems," how would you respond to a pair of distraught parents?

2. In recent years, toy manufacturers have, with increasing frequency, sought the advice of psychologists. What general recom-
mendations would you favor in toy design that would facilitate
cognitive development of young children.

3. As indicated in the text, parents are sending children to preschools today more so than in years past. If advising parents on
how to choose a preschool, what characteristics would you tell them
to look for.

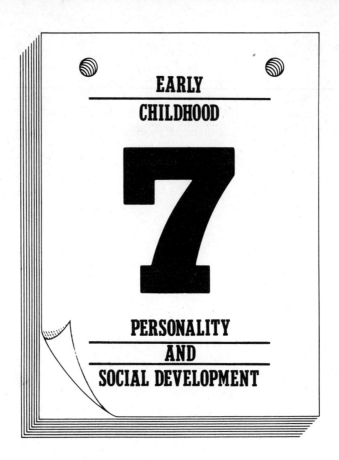

EARLY

CHILDHOOD

7

PERSONALITY

AND

SOCIAL DEVELOPMENT

INTEGRATOR

In Chapter 5, the theories of Freud and Erikson were introduced.
These are continued in Chapter 7 as we consider personality and
social development in early childhood. These theories are important
in later life-span periods also, so they will be covered again in
Chapters 9, 11, 13, 15, and 17. The issue of sex typing is considered in some depth. Sex-role identification will be shown to
be a potent variable in personality and social functioning for
people of all ages and will emerge as an important variable many
times throughout this text. Children's fears, play behavior,
friendships, and personality characteristics serve as a medium in
which the interplay between heredity and environment, already considered in earlier chapters, can be clearly seen. Once again, the
relative importance of genetic endowment and environmental factors
is considered.

OVERVIEW

Theoretical Perspectives on Personality in Early Childhood

The early-childhood period is critical for the development of personality. The first section considers two major theoretical perspectives on this development, those of Freud and Erikson. Freud

proposed that children of 3 or 4 years of age are in the phallic stage, indicating a shift in the primary zone of pleasure from the anal area to the genital area. Little boys identify with their fathers through the resolution of the Oedipus complex and its resulting castration complex. Similarly, girls identify with their mothers through resolution of the Electra complex and penis envy. Such identification with the parents is crucial for the development of the superego. The superego develops as the child introjects the parent's personality.

Erik Erikson's psychosocial approach stresses a shift from an attachment to parents to identification with parents. As the child identifies with the parents it faces the crisis of initiative versus guilt. Successful resolution of this crisis and the previous crisis of autonomy versus shame allows the child to achieve some detachment from the parents.

Both Freud and Erikson stress the importance of identification as a process by which children acquire parental characteristics. This process seems to be enhanced when the child becomes aware of similarities between parents and child.

Key terms in this section:

phallic stage	superego
Oedipus complex	introjection
castration complex	initiative versus guilt
Electra complex	detachment
penis envy	identification

Sex Typing

Sex typing, the process by which children acquire the behavior and attitudes regarded by their culture as characteristically masculine or feminine, is a crucial factor in personality development. It involves the motives, emotions, and values that people use to direct their lives from infancy to the grave.

Actual sex differences begin to emerge in childhood in motor skills and field independence. Such differences alone do not, however, account for sex typing. Other factors which influence this process include cultural norms as well as biological factors. Theoretical explanations of sex typing thus represent a full range of cultural and biological orientations and include: (1) biological theory, (2) psychoanalytic theory, (3) social learning theory which stresses three mechanisms--socialization, observation, and reciprocal role, and (4) cognitive developmental theory proposed by Kohlberg. A number of problems persist with each of these theoretical orientations, and none of them fully explains sex typing.

American culture promotes clear sex-role stereotypes which children learn early. The degree to which children adopt traditional sex

93

roles is influenced by factors such as socioeconomic level, parent-child interactions, parental warmth, father's behavior, and other variables such as mass-media models, playmates and nursery school experiences.

Key terms in this section:

sex typing
field independence
biological theory
psychoanalytic theory
social learning theory

cognitive developmental theory
socialization
observation
reciprocal role

Children's Fears

The years from 2 to 6 seem to harbor the greatest number of new fears. These may be caused by actual events, parental overprotection, anxiety over personal injury, or guilt. With increasing age, fears decrease in number and type. Gender and socioeconomic status are also related to expression of fears.

Attempts to overcome fears using ridicule, coercion, logical explanation, or ignoring them have no positive effect and may in fact aggravate the problem. The best ways to help children overcome fears involve learning procedures in which the child is an active participant.

Child-Rearing Practices and Personality Development

Children's environment has a strong impact upon their personality development and parents represent a crucial facet of that environment. Three major dimensions of children's personality, aggression, dependency, and passivity, have received considerable study. Aggression is highly influenced by modeling and imitation and by the fact that it is often rewarded by attention of parents and other children. Studies on the effects of television indicate that children are more likely to act aggressively after viewing media violence and are more accepting of violence as a legitimate problem-solving strategy.

Passivity and dependency are lifelong traits that do not emerge until the school age period. It is suggested that dependency may result from frustration in infancy by overprotective domineering parents.

Prosocial or altruistic behaviors are actions that are intended to aid or benefit another person or group of people without the actor's anticipation of external rewards. The development of these positive personality traits is not related to socioeconomic status or gender but is related to age and parental modeling, emphasis on the needs of others, and expectations. Development of prosocial behavior appears to relate more to how parents feel about their children

94

rather than what parents do.

Styles of child rearing have changed regularly over the years, and general "rules of parenting" are always subject to widespread exceptions. Nonetheless, some broad categories of child rearing practices have been differentiated as having troublesome or more-positive effects. Baumrind has described three such categories: the authoritarian, the permissive, and the authoritative. The authoritative parents, who have reasonable expectations and standards for their children, seem to have the best-adjusted children. Influential contemporary voices in parent education include Benjamin Spock (<u>Baby and child care</u>), Haim Ginott (<u>Between parent and child</u>), and Thomas Gordon (<u>P.E.T., parent effectiveness training</u>). All three stress an authoritative approach to child rearing.

Key terms in this section:

aggression   authoritarian parent
passivity   permissive parent
dependency   authoritative parent
prosocial (altruistic) behavior

Play and Friendship in Early Childhood

Play is the "work of the young" through which physical growth and skill is achieved and learning about life is accomplished. Parten described six types of play, listed in Table 7-1, which included unoccupied behavior, onlooker play, solitary play, parallel activity , associative play, and cooperative play. Recent data indicate that social-class-significant social events such as television and decreasing family size may be changing children's play patterns. The age mixture within the group of children and the settings can also affect play style. Setting changes can lead to more functional play or constructive play.

Play can be an effective means of coping with stress and has been used to aid intellectual development of children in fantasy play and sociodramatic play groups when compared to a fantasy discussion and control groups. Imaginary playmates are a normal manifestation of childhood and underscore the relationship between play, coping, and intellectual functioning.

The function of play has been explained in various ways by different theorists. Piaget's cognitive theory views it as a way to learn about new and complex objects and events. Freud's psychoanalytic view saw it as helping ego strength, while Thorndike saw it as learned behavior.

Friendships become increasingly important as the child progresses through early childhood. Selman and Selman have delineated five stages in children's thinking about friendships. Stage 0, stage of momentary playmateship, and stage 1, one-way assistance, are typical of early childhood.

The tendency to develop friendships appears related to similarity in activity level, maternal attachment, and early notions of reciprocity. The study of friendships is part of a new branch of developmental study called social cognition.

Key terms in this section:

unoccupied behavior
onlooker play
solitary play
parallel play
associative play
cooperative play
functional play
constructive play
fantasy play group

sociodramatic play group
fantasy discussion group
imaginary playmates
stage of momentary playmateship
 (0)
stage of one-way assistance (1)
reciprocity in friendship
social cognition

LEARNING OBJECTIVES

1. Describe the general nature of the phallic stage of psycho-sexual development. (p. 220)

2. Describe the process by which, according to Freud, boys identify with their fathers. (p. 220)

3. Describe the process by which, according to Freud, girls identify with their mothers. (pp. 220-221)

4. Explain the process by which the superego is said to develop. (p. 221)

5. Describe Erikson's crisis of initiative and how identification leads to detachment. (pp. 221-222)

6. List some sex differences which begin to emerge in early childhood. (p. 223)

7. Explain the concept of sex typing and describe four theories of how it comes about. (pp. 223-226)

   Sex-typing:

   a.

   b.

   c.

d.

8. Describe problems associated with each of the four theories
   of sex typing. (pp. 226-227)

   a.

   b.

   c.

   d.

9. Describe the influence of each of the following on the development of traditional sex-role attitudes in children. (pp. 227-23

   Socioeconomic level

   Parent/child interactions

   Father's behavior

   Mass media

10. Discuss the factors that are related to the increase in fears in early childhood. (pp. 231-232)

11. Describe effective and noneffective procedures for helping children overcome their fears. (pp. 232-233)

12. Discuss factors which seem related to the development of passivity and aggression in children. (pp. 234-237)

13. Define prosocial behavior and discuss factors related to its development. (pp. 237-239)

14. List and describe the three prototypes of parental practices described by Baumrind. (pp. 240-241)

   a.

   b.

c.

15. Briefly summarize the emphasis of the following contemporary voices on parenting. (pp. 241-242)

Dr. B. Spock

H. Ginott

T. Gordon

16. Describe the type of play denoted by each of the following terms. (pp. 243-245)

   a. Unoccupied behavior

   b. Onlooker play

   c. Solitary play

   d. Parallel play

   e. Associative play

f. Cooperative play

g. Functional play

h. Constructive play

17. Describe how play patterns are affected by age mixture and setting. (pp. 244-246)

18. Review data indicating that play can have a beneficial impact on intellectual functioning. (pp. 245-246)

19. Describe the functions of play according to the following theoretical orientations. (pp. 246-247)

Cognitive

Psychoanalytic

20. Describe the early development of friendships as proposed by Selman and Selman. (p. 248)

21. List the factors which contribute to a child's tendency to form friendships. (pp. 249-250)

SELF TEST A

Circle the letter of the choice that completes each item.

1. According to Freud, during the phallic stage boys must resolve their: (a) Oedipus complex; (b) Electra complex; (c) initiative crisis; (d) penis envy.

2. Erikson's third crisis describes a conflict between: (a) initiative and guilt; (b) attachment and detachment; (c) detachment and identification; (d) autonomy and shame.

3. The process by which children acquire behavior and attitudes regarded by their culture as masculine or feminine is called: (a) identification; (b) sex typing; (c) introjection; (d) detachment.

4. Recent educational theories have shifted to the view that strongly differentiated sex roles: (a) enhance intellectual and psychological development of children; (b) impede intellectual and psychological development of children; (c) have little or no effect on the intellectual and psychological development of children; (d) increase healthy competition in the classroom.

5. Tom, a 27-year-old mechanic, is a prototype, traditionally masculine individual. He strongly approves of and fosters feminine behavior in Alisa, his 5-year-old daughter. According to social learning theory, this is a case of sex typing through: (a) socialization; (b) observation; (c) identification; (d) reciprocal role.

6. Which of the following has not been found to be related to children's sex-role attitudes? (a) socioeconomic status; (b) father's behavior; (c) religion; (d) parental warmth.

7. Bill and Marjorie tend to be detached, controlling, and less warm than most parents. Baumrind would classify these parents as: (a) permissive; (b) authoritarian; (c) authoritative; (d) rejecting.

8. The best method for helping children overcome fears is to: (a) ridicule the child's fear; (b) logically explain that the fear is unfounded; (c) encourage the child to actively cope with the fear; (d) ignore the fear.

9. Carrie spends her time during free play at her preschool playing with Tom and Joan. As they play, they talk excitedly about their game and share materials as they each take turns and imitate each others' action. This type of play is called: (a) associative play; (b) cooperative play; (c) parallel play; (d) solitary play.

10. Bob, a 4-year-old, says that John is his friend because he lives next door and has a tricycle. Bob cannot see John's point of view in their relationship. Bob is in the _____ stage of friendship development. (a) reciprocity; (b) materialistic; (c) momentary playmateship; (d) one-way assistance.

PRACTICE EXERCISES

Completion

Supply the words or phrases that best complete these sentences.

1. According to the theory of the _____ _____, a 3- to 6-year-old boy lavishes love and affection with decidedly sexual overtones on his mother, thus competing with his father for the mother's love and affection. The counter-

    part for a little girl is the _____ _____.

2. By identifying with the parent of the same sex, children actually take the parent's personality into their own. In

    psychoanalytic terms, this is called _____.

3. According to Erikson, the basic conflict for preschool children

is between _____, which enables them to plan

and carry out activities, and _____ over what they
want to do.

4. _____ _____ is the process by which children
acquire the behavior and attitudes regarded by their culture
as characteristically masculine or feminine.

5. Margaret Mead's description of three New Guinea tribes indi-

cates that sex typing is not wholly _____ but

that it is determined by _____ expectations as
well.

6. _____ theory maintains that sex typing is an

indirect result of anatomic differences, while _____

_____ theory postulates three mechanisms by which
children acquire sex roles from the environment. These are:

_____, _____, and

_____ _____.

7. The pressure on children to conform to sex-role expectations

is _____ _____ in the lower socioeconomic groups.

8. Both boys and girls report being kissed more by the parent

of the _____ sex, and they tend to see the

_____- _____ parent as "less benevolent and more
frustrating" (Rothbart and Maccoby 1966).

9. _____ tends to perpetuate outdated stereotypes by
showing males to be aggressive and constructive, while showing
females as dependent and inactive.

10. The years from _____ to _____ seem to harbor the
greatest number of new fears.

11. The best ways to help children overcome fears--which they are

usually eager to shed--involve _____

_____.

12. Bandura, Ross, and Ross have demonstrated that _____ aggression makes children more aggressive and more

    _____ of aggression as a problem-solving technique.

13. Passivity is more than inactivity: it is the state of being

    _____; it is the
    failure to initiate behavior. Dependency is the opposite of

    _____-_____.

14. Actions intended to help others without expectation of external

    reward by the actor are called _____ or

    _____ behavior.

15. _____ parents try to control their children's
    behavior and attitudes and make them conform to a set and

    usually absolute standard of conduct. _____
    parents make few demands, allowing their children to regulate

    their own activities as much as possible. _____
    parents try to direct their children's activities rationally,
    with attention to the issues rather than the children's fears
    of punishment or loss of love.

True-False

Circle T if the statement is true, F if the statement is false.

T F 1. Barnes has found that children today play less socially
        than Parten's group did 40 years ago.

T F 2. Saltz, Dixon, and Johnson found that IQ scores increased
        most for children who were in play groups.

T F 3. Psychoanalytic theory proposes that play is an important
        means of consolidating and enlarging new concepts.

T F 4. Young children (3-7 years) tend to think about only what
        they want from a friendship.

T F 5. Freud proposes that boys identify with their fathers to
        reduce penis envy.

T F 6. The superego is much like a conscience and is acquired
        through detachment from the parents.

T F 7. The process of identification involves acquiring many
        of the characteristics of another person.

T F 8. Sex typing is stronger in America than in most other nations.

T F 9. Evidence indicates that sex typing is entirely the result of cultural factors.

T F 10. None of the theories of sex typing provides a completely satisfactory explanation of the process.

Word Scrambler

Unscramble the ten items. Then arrange the circled letters to complete the sentence below.

1.

E D U S O P I

Freudian complex for boys

2.

H L P A I L C

Psychosexual stage in early childhood

3.

I P S E N

Envy which is the basis of identification in girls

4.

J O T I C I E N N T R O

Psychoanalytic term for children taking parents' personality as their own

5.

I Z O S N C I L O I A A T

Social-learning-theory process of sex typing

6.

T R S E N V A B O O I

Social-learning-theory process of sex typing through imitation

7.

A V I P T S I S Y

Being done to instead of doing

8. _ _ O _ _ _ _ _ _ _ _ _
   U I A N A R T T A H I R O

   Highly controlling parenting style

9. _ _ _ _ _ O _ _ _ _ _ _
   T U A A R T O H I I T E V

   Parenting style yielding the most well-adjusted children

10. _ _ _ O _ _ _ _
    E P L R L A L A

   Play which is independent while children are near each other

   If resolved successfully, Erikson's third crisis will give

   the child a sense of _ _ _ _ _ _ _ _ _ _ .

SELF TEST B

Circle the letter of the choice that completes each item.

1. According to Freud, a female has a lifelong psychological defect
which he called: (a) penis envy; (b) Electra complex; (c) Oedipus
complex; (d) castration complex.

2. In psychoanalytic terms, when a child identifies with the same-
sex parent, the child is: (a) imitating; (b) introjecting; (c)
imprinting; (d) socializing.

3. Although United States society is less rigid than many others
in its sex-role definitions, it still consistently: (a) overvalues
abilities that fall within female competence; (b) undervalues
abilities that fall within male competence; (c) undervalues abilities that fall within female competence; (d) values male and female
competence equally.

4. Joan is from a lower socioeconomic class and Mary is from a
middle-class group. Both girls are 7 years old. If offered both
sex-appropriate and sex-inappropriate toys we could predict that:
(a) both girls would prefer sex-appropriate toys; (b) Joan would
choose "girls' toys" but Mary would not; (c) both girls would
choose sex-inappropriate toys; (d) Mary would choose "girls toys"
but Joan would not.

5. Children apparently harbor the largest number of new fears
during the years from: (a) 6 to 12; (b) 2 to 6; (c) 4 to 8;
(d) 8 to 12.

6. Many studies clearly show that after viewing violence on TV:
(a) some normal children will act more aggressively; (b) all normal
children are unaffected; (c) only deviant children will act more
aggressively; (d) children are agitated but less aggressive.

7. Today's fashion in child rearing can be described by the statement: (a) Father knows best. (b) Children know what is best for
them. (c) Parents probably know best--but children know something
too. (d) Parents know very little, and professional training is
crucial.

8. Parents who are relatively more detached, more controlling,
and less warm than other parents would be called: (a) permissive;
(b) authoritarian; (c) authoritative; (d) hostile-abusing.

9. Dr. Benjamin Spock was highly influenced by the theories of:
(a) Freud; (b) Rogers; (c) Erikson; (d) Jung.

10. According to _____ theory, play is a means of working through
problems and developing ego strength. (a) ego; (b) cognitive;
(c) learning; (c) psychoanalytic.

VIGNETTES

1. A feminist friend has just stated that all sex-typing is based
on cultural norms, set by men, which degrade and subjugate women.
How would you respond if you wished to disagree?

2. The parents of 5-year-old Billy have approached you for help.
Billy has developed a terrible fear of the drain in his bathtub.
It is very difficult to get him to bathe. His parents have tried
to explain that there is no danger and have tried to shame him into
more suitable behavior. What would you do?

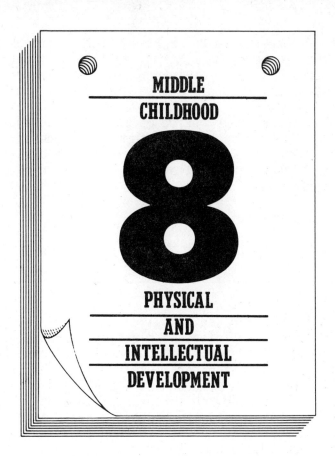

MIDDLE
CHILDHOOD

8

PHYSICAL
AND
INTELLECTUAL
DEVELOPMENT

INTEGRATOR

In Chapter 8, the discussion of physical development begun in
Chapters 3 and 6 will be continued with emphasis placed upon the
physical and motor development of schoolchildren as well as specific
health hazards faced during this (the middle-childhood) period. The
next major sections will continue to trace the unfolding intellectual
capacities of children as they enter Piaget's stage of concrete
operations in preparation for formal operations which will be considered in Chapter 10. The problem of intelligence testing introduced in Chapter 4 is expanded to include concerns of creativity,
correlates to cognitive functioning, and needs of gifted children.
Of special interest is the introduction of Kohlberg's stages of
moral development, which will be further examined in Chapter 10.

OVERVIEW

Physical and Motor Development in Middle Childhood

Between the ages of 6 and 12, physical growth is less rapid than
it was during the infancy and toddlerhood periods, and a wide range
of individual differences is the rule. In general, children from
more-affluent environments mature earlier and are bigger. Girls,

who attain the adolescent growth spurt earlier, overtake boys in height and weight in about the sixth grade. Prediction of adult height is often based upon x-ray measures of the degree of bone ossification (skeletal or bone age).

Motor development during this period is marked by advances in size, strength, and coordination. Male and female development during this period show clear differences which raise the question of the degree to which cultural expectations and physical differences promote such sex differences.

Key terms in this section:

ossification   bone age

Intellectual Development During Middle Childhood

According to Piaget, children become operational in thinking between the ages of 5 and 7. Their use of symbols to carry out operations allows them to be more proficient at classifying, number manipulation, and conservation. Decreasing egocentrism allows the child to understand the viewpoints of others more readily, and primitive concepts such as realism, animism, and artificialism gradually drop out. Throughout this period, children begin to conserve and exhibit horizontal decalage as they gradually extend this skill from conservation of substance to weight and then to volume. As the children begin to achieve conservation solutions, their justifications can be based upon reversibility, identity, or compensation. Increasing facility in conservation is closely allied with improving skill in transitivity.

Key terms in this section:

operations   substance, weight, volume
realism   conservation
animism   compensation
artificialism   transitivity
horizontal decalage

Moral Development in Schoolchildren

The next section of Chapter 8 deals with moral development in schoolchildren, emphasizing the work of Piaget and Kohlberg. Both of these theorists regard moral development as a process that coincides with cognitive development. Maturity in moral judgments must be based upon cognitive maturity.

For Piaget, moral development progresses through two stages. Initially, children are in stage 1, morality of constraint or heteronomous morality, which is characterized by rigid conceptions of rules, intentionality, punishment, and justice. After interacting with other people who hold differing views and experiencing advancing cognitive development, children advance toward stage 2, morality of cooperation or autonomous morality. Table 8-2 compares the child's viewpoint in these two stages on six important points including general point of view, intentionality, rules respect for authority, expiatory versus reciprocal punishment, and immanent justice.

Kohlberg has expanded Piaget's view of morality and has postulated six types of moral reasoning presented in Table 8-4. These six types are organized on three levels: premorality, conventional morality, and self-accepted moral principles.

Research which has attempted to verify the theoretical formulations of Piaget and Kohlberg regarding moral development has provided only partial support. This is also true for other theories which have been advanced to account for moral development. Social learning theory postulates that children acquire moral values by modeling and being rewarded by their parents. Psychoanalytic theory sees identification with the parents resulting from resolution of Oedipus and Electra complexes as the crucial mechanism. In both instances, research has provided only partial support.

Robert Selman sees role-taking skill as crucial in moral reasoning development. He has described five stages (0 through 4) of role-taking ability which are related to Piaget's cognitive stages and Kohlberg's moral-reasoning stages. Comparison of Selman's, Piaget's, and Kohlberg's stages is provided in Table 8-6. Studies with delinquent youth emphasize the relationship between both role-taking ability and referential communication ability and moral reasoning. Values clarification is an approach to advancing moral reasoning by encouraging children to analyze the values by which they live.

Key terms in this section:

morality of constraint	immanent justice
(heteronomous morality)	premorality
morality of cooperation	conventional morality
(autonomous morality)	self-accepted moral principles
expiatory punishment	referential communication
reciprocal punishment	values clarification

Development of Schoolchildren's Communication Ability

Six-year-old children exhibit fairly sophisticated language skills. They use complex grammar and have a vocabulary of some 2500 words. Despite this skill 6-year-olds still have not mastered syntax and will continue to develop in this area up to and possibly beyond 9 years of age. Communication ability improves as egocentrism diminishes.

Measuring Intelligence in Schoolchildren

The intelligence of schoolchildren is measured by both individual and group tests. Popular scales include: the Stanford-Binet, the Wechsler Intelligence Scale for Children (WISC), the Otis-Lennon Mental Ability Test, Primary Level, and the Large-Thorndike Multi-Level Battery. Cultural influence on test performance is a singularly major issue facing test designers. Recognizing the impossibility of designing a culture-free test, test makers have tried to produce culture-fair tests, which is itself a monumentally difficult task. Comparison of test scores of black and white American children underscores the problem of cultural influences on test performance. Lower scores for blacks may reflect a genetic factor as proposed in Jensenism or distinct cultural factors as is maintained by supporters of the System of Multicultural Pluralistic Assessment (SOMPA).

Key terms in this section:

culture-free tests
culture-fair tests
Jensenism

System of Multicultural
    Pluralistic Assessment (SOMPA)

Correlates of Cognitive Functioning and Gifted Children

The next section of Chapter 8 deals with correlates of cognitive functioning. Temperament, impulsivity versus reflectivity, gender, and parental child-rearing practices are listed as important variables. Identification of gifted children is a major challenge which researchers have approached using retrospective studies. A distinction between divergent thinking and convergent thinking is noted. Creativity, based upon the former, is not easily measured and is not assessed using the standard intelligence scales. The University of Southern California Tests from the Aptitude Research Project (ARP) and the Torrance Tests of Creative Thinking may better measure creative aptitude. A number of family influences including social class, number of siblings, spacing of siblings, gender, conformity, and child-rearing practices, have been related to creativity in children.

When both intelligence and creativity are assessed four patterns may result: Children may score high or low on both or they may score high on one and low on the other. Intelligence and creativity are seen, therefore, as separate constructs.

Key terms in this section:

impulsivity vs. reflectivity
divergent vs. convergent
    thinking
creativity

USC tests from Aptitude Research
    Project (ARP)
Torrance Tests of Creative
    Thinking

Children in School

The final section of this chapter deals with the impact of the school on the child. The child's school experience is influenced by various factors: type of classroom (open or traditional); teachers' attitudes, which can lead to a self-fulfilling prophecy; socioeconomic status; sex; and cultural membership.

Other special concerns related to school include educating handicapped children. Controversy over mainstreaming special students is prevalent.

Learning disabilities can be very specific or rather vague. Minimal brain dysfunction is a term used to refer to general disability of unknown origin. Tests such as the WISC and WPPSI and the Illinois Test of Psycholinguistic Abilities (ITPA) have been developed to help assess specific disabilities. School phobia is a problem that has received recent attention. Neurotic and characterological types of school phobia have been distinguished.

Key terms in this section:

open classroom   school phobia
self-fulfilling prophecy   neurotic school phobia
mainstreaming   characterological school phobia
minimal brain dysfunction

LEARNING OBJECTIVES

1. Describe the differences in physical appearance between pre-school and school-aged children. (p. 256)

2. Describe the process used to predict adult height using x-ray technology. (p. 256)

3. Identify the major health problems of children under the age of 14. (pp. 257-259)

4. Explain why poverty is considered to be the most serious health problem among American children today. (p. 259)

5. Describe the sex differences that occur in motor development during the school years. (p. 260)

6. Discuss genetic and cultural factors which may contribute to sex differences in motor development of schoolchildren. (pp. 260-261)

7. Briefly explain what Piaget means when he says a child becomes "operational" between ages 5 and 7. (p. 261)

8. Realism is divided into three stages. Describe each of them. (p. 262)

   a.

   b.

   c.

9. Explain what is meant by animism and describe four stages of animistic thinking. (p. 262)

   Animism:

   Stage 1

   Stage 2

   Stage 3

   Stage 4

10. Describe artificialism in children's thinking and describe three stages of artificialism. (pp. 262-263)

Artificialism:

Stage 1

Stage 2

Stage 3

11. Discuss the effects of culture on conservation ability.
    (pp. 263-264)

12. Explain the concept of horizontal decalage. (p. 264)

13. Describe three types of justification children give for their
    conservation responses. (p. 264)

14. Discuss the relationship between conservation and transitivity. (p. 264)

15. Explain the cognitive developmental approach to moral thinking. (pp. 264-265)

16. Contrast the morality of constraint and the morality of cooperation. (pp. 265-267)

17. List and explain Kohlberg's six stages of moral reasoning. (p. 269)

    a.

    b.

    c.

    d.

e.

f.

18. Describe the social-learning-theory and psychoanalytic approaches to moral development and summarize research results testing these approaches. (pp. 268-271)

19. List Selman's four stages of the development of role-taking skills. (pp. 271-274)

a.

b.

c.

d.

20. Describe the implications of role-taking ability and referential communication for moral reasoning. (p. 274)

21. Explain what is involved in values clarification. (p. 275)

22. Discuss the impact of egocentrism on communication skills of the preschool child. (pp. 277-278)

23. Briefly discuss the difficulties involved in designing culture-free or culture-fair tests. (p. 279)

24. Give some reasons why black children's IQ is about 15 points below that of whites. (pp. 279-282)

25. Describe the impact of each of the following on intelligence test performance. (pp. 282-285)

    a. Temperament

    b. Impulsivity vs. reflectivity

c. Sex

d. Parental child-rearing practices

26. Discuss the problem of identifying gifted children. (pp. 285-288)

27. Contrast convergent and divergent thinking and discuss the importance of this distinction for assessing creativity. (p. 288)

28. Describe factors in the home that contribute to creativity. (pp. 289-290)

29. Describe the relationships that have been found between intelligence and creativity. (pp. 290-291)

30. Discuss four factors which affect the school experience of children. (pp. 291-293)

31. Explain the self-fulfilling prophecy and tell what implications it has for minority-group and poor children. (p. 294)

32. Briefly explain the following conditions and indicate how they may be treated. (pp. 295-299)

Bilingual children

Learning disabilities

Minimal brain dysfunction

School phobia

SELF TEST A

Circle the letter of the choice that completes each item.

1. Compared to the preschool years, children in the middle years show: (a) very slow growth change; (b) a tremendous change in

121

growth; (c) a very narrow range in height; (d) a stable overall weight with a height increase.

2. The most accurate assessment by which a child's ultimate adult height can be predicted requires the use of: (a) skeletal age; (b) channelwise progression; (c) percentage relationship; (d) ultrasound.

3. The leading cause of death among children today is: (a) tuberculosis; (b) accidents; (c) drowning; (d) polio.

4. One of the implications of studies of physical development is that: (a) there are no longer any major health or disease problems in the United states; (b) boys and girls differ appreciably in their motor abilities in the middle years and thus should have separate physical education; (c) there is no good reason to separate boys and girls for physical education in the middle years; (d) sex differences in physical skill are genetically based, and therefore boys and girls should have physical-education classes which emphasize different skills.

5. Bill believes that anything that moves or can be moved is alive. To him bicycles, automobiles, and chairs are alive. Bill exhibits: (a) Stage 3 of animism; (b) Stage 1 of realism; (c) Stage 2 of artificialism; (d) Stage 2 of animism.

6. Piaget termed the stage at which children become able to use symbols to carry out mental activities the stage of: (a) concrete operations; (b) conservation; (c) animism; (d) symbolism.

7. In his theory of conservation, Piaget stressed that children would learn the concept: (a) if they were given adequate training; (b) when they were cognitively mature enough; (c) at certain chronological ages; (d) and apply it to all objects at once.

8. A new approach being used to help children make moral judgments is called: (a) animism; (b) values clarification; (c) transitivity; (d) referential communication.

9. Which of the following is true of creative children who score low in intelligence tests: (a) They make up for their low intellectual status with social success. (b) They have much self-confidence and self-esteem. (c) They have the most trouble in school. (d) They tend to be "teacher's pets."

10. Neurotic school phobia occurs most frequently in: (a) fourth-graders to eighth-graders; (b) kindergartners to fourth-graders; (c) ninth-graders to twelfth-graders; (d) preschoolers.

PRACTICE EXERCISES

Completion

Supply the words or phrases that best complete these sentences.

1. Children from affluent communities are somewhat _____
    than those from lower socioeconomic groups. This is due to

    their better _____.

2. The process of bone formation, or _____, con-
    tinues until the individual achieves full growth, at about

    the age of _____.

3. Low-income minority-group children have disproportionately

    high levels of _____ and _____.

4. The leading cause of death among children is _____.

5. Govatos (1959) found that boys and girls of similar size

    tended to do equally well in _____ and _____,

    but boys generally outdid girls in _____ and

    _____.

6. Sometimes between 5 and 7 years of age, children become what
    Piaget calls operational; that is, they become able to use

    _____ to carry out _____.

7. When children confuse psychological events with objective
    reality and see names, pictures, thoughts, and feelings as

    actual entities, they are in the throes of _____.

8. Young children's egocentric tendency to endow inanimate ob-
    jects with life, consciousness, and will--characteristics

    they themselves possess--is called _____.

9. Egocentric children's feelings that they, or other human
    beings, have created everything in the world (including the

    sun, the moon, and the stars) is known as _____.

10. Before children master any type of conservation problem, they

go through three stages. In the first, they _____ _____

_____. The second stage in conservation is transi-

tional, during which children _____. In the
third and final stage in conservation, children conserve and
give logical justifications for their answers. These justi-

fications may take the form of _____,

_____, or _____.

Matching

In the blank to the left of each definition, write the letter that
indicates the term defined.

_____ 1. Recognition of a relationship between two objects by
           knowing the relationship between each of them and a
           third

_____ 2. Kohlberg's most primitive type of moral reasoning

_____ 3. Kohlberg's highest level of morality

_____ 4. Piaget's first moral stage

_____ 5. Technique to enhance moral reasoning

_____ 6. Major block to effective communication

_____ 7. Proposes that lower black IQ scores are genetically
           based

_____ 8. Program used to place special-education students and
           which considers cultural background

_____ 9. Tendency to respond slowly and carefully after careful
           consideration of a problem

_____ 10. Based on divergent thinking

a. values clarification   f. creativity
b. punishment orientation   g. transitivity
c. Jensenism   h. egocentrism
d. SOMPA   i. self-accepted principles
e. reflectivity   j. heteronomous morality

True-False

Circle T if the statement is true, F if the statement is false.

T F   1. Accidents are the major leading cause of death for
           children aged 1 to 14 years.

124

T F 2. In the third stage of realism, children believe that dreams are unreal images seen with the eyes.

T F 3. The order in which children conserve elements is substance, weight, and volume.

T F 4. Piaget stresses that children will conserve only when their cognitive systems have matured.

T F 5. Heteronomous-stage children believe in reciprocal punishment, flexible rules, and immanent justice.

T F 6. Research data clearly support the moral-development theory proposed by the social-learning approach.

T F 7. Referential communication involves effective verbal transmission of visual information.

T F 8. Only the Wechsler scales have been shown to be culturally free.

T F 9. Blacks tend to fall behind in intelligence-test scores at about age 2 to 3.

T F 10. Data indicate that home environment can affect IQ test performance.

T F 11. Temperament, level of impulsivity, and gender all influence cognitive functioning.

T F 12. For school-aged children, mothers may have more influence on their cognitive functioning.

T F 13. Conceiving novel responses which effectively apply to a problem is called convergent thinking.

T F 14. "Model" students score high in intelligence and low in creativity.

T F 15. School phobia in kindergartners is typically neurotic.

SELF TEST B

Circle the letter of the choice that completes each item.

1. If we assess a child's bone age, we will be using x-rays to assess: (a) the mean bone length in the extremities; (b) the degree of fat in proportion to muscle tissue; (c) the degree of bone ossification; (d) the level of bone fusion in the skull.

2. The most serious health problem for children today is: (a) tuberculosis; (b) accidents; (c) poverty; (d) hepatitis.

3. In terms of motor development, boys: (a) improve in performance from ages 5 to 17, while girls improve in the early school years; (b) improve the same as girls do, from ages 5 to 17; (c) do not

improve until the age of 13, while girls improve before that age; (d) are always slightly ahead of girls.

4. Govatos (1959) found that boys and girls of similar size tended to: (a) differ in running and jumping abilities; (b) do equally well in running and jumping abilities; (c) do equally well in throwing and kicking abilities; (d) do equally well on all motor tasks.

5. One likely reason that girls may slow down in motor skills at age 13 is because: (a) it is at this age that "tomboyishness" is discouraged; (b) they have grown too tall to be coordinated; (c) physical maturity slows down at this time; (d) of the onset of menstruation.

6. Joan is very disturbed because she has just met another girl her age named Joan. The problem is that the girls have different skin colors; one is black and one is white. Joan is very uncertain as to how this can be because she is in: (a) Stage 2 of artificialism; (b) Stage 2 of realism; (c) Stage 1 of realism; (d) Stage 4 of animism.

7. Piaget's second stage of morality in schoolchildren--the morality of cooperation--is characterized by: (a) moral rigidity; (b) animism; (c) moral flexibility; (d) belief in immanent justice.

8. Bill thinks that a person should behave because that is what a good boy or girl does. He seeks to please others. This type of moral reasoning is found in Kholberg's: (a) conventional morality level; (b) premoral level; (c) principled morality level; (d) morality of contract.

9. A test that tries to eliminate all cultural content is called a: (a) cross-cultural test; (b) culture-fair test; (c) culture-free test; (d) projective test.

10. The mainstreaming approach to education: (a) places handicapped children in regular classes with normal children; (b) places handicapped children in special segregated classes for most of the day; (c) gives special emphasis to children with special needs; (d) identifies gifted children for accelerated coursework.

VIGNETTES

1. At a PTA meeting a group of parents are expressing great concern over the fact that their fifth-grade sons and daughters engage in gym activities together. The thrust of their argument is that boys and girls are so different in physical skill and interest that separate gym classes are needed to provide the proper types of activities. As an expert, what would you respond?

2. Bob and Louise Crenshaw have come to you very upset because their second-grader has been caught stealing. The Crenshaws are worried because they believe that they must have modeled immoral behavior for their child but cannot see how this is true. Their child justified the act of taking candy from a store by saying that painful hunger was the motivating factor. How might you calm the Crenshaw's concerns.

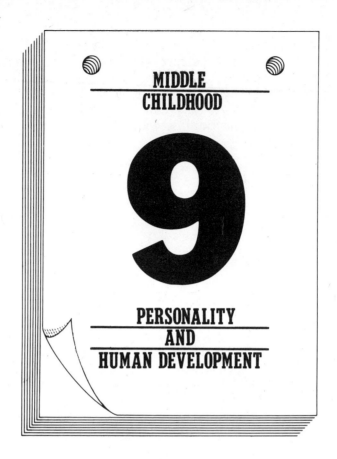

MIDDLE
CHILDHOOD

9

PERSONALITY
AND
HUMAN DEVELOPMENT

INTEGRATOR

Chapter 9 will extend the discussions begun in Chapters 5 and 7 of personality and social development of school-aged children. The theoretical formulations of Freud and Erikson will again be prominent in the discussion, which is expanded to include the impact of peers as self-concepts develop. The role of prejudice and sex typing is considered, as is the role of family life. Development of self-concept will be a major issue of adolescence to be considered in Chapter 11. The role of peers, introduced here, will also be a major issue for adolescent development.

OVERVIEW

Theoretical Perspectives on Personality Development

Freud termed the elementary school years the latency period because he erroneously thought it to be a period of sexual quiescence. In fact children's sexual interest during this period (the years from 6 to 12) is significant, though Oedipal and sex-role conflicts are generally resolved at this point. The child develops numerous defense mechanisms to uphold ego strength. These include: regression, repression, sublimation, projection, and reaction formation.

Erikson views the school years as the period during which children learn the skills of their culture. Productivity becomes important to the child as he becomes a "worker instead of a player." The central crisis then centers around industry versus inferiority.

Key terms in this section:

latency period	projection
regression	reaction formation
repression	industry vs. inferiority
sublimation	

The Society of Childhood

Although children today live and think differently from those of years gone by, they continue to pass down traditional lore, rhymes, humor, and games to those younger than themselves. Children are great traditionalists, playing games and engaging in pastimes that have been popular for literally thousands of years. Children's humor reflects their continuing interest in sexuality and aids them in dealing with issues they cannot readily understand or which arouse anxiety.

The peer group assumes an increasingly important role during middle childhood as the child spends more and more time away from the family and in the company of friends. The peer group serves numerous functions such as providing information about the world, influencing the child's self-concept, and serving as a sounding board for parent-derived values. Despite its powerful influence, there is considerable variation in the degree to which children conform to peer group standards.

Sociometric methods, particularly the sociogram, help psychologists identify popular and unpopular children. Popular children tend to be healthy, vigorous, poised, capable of initiative but with restraint, dependable, affectionate, considerate, and original thinkers. They have generally moderate levels of self-esteem. Unpopular children are often withdrawn, or rebellious, grudging, anxious, uncertain, and prone to alienate others by their behavior or appearance.

Adults can have significant impact upon peer groups. Children behave quite differently when the adult leader is authoritarian, democratic or laissez faire. Some countries--for example, Russia and Israel--have used peer groups to socialize children to further the goals of society.

Friendships progress through stages 1 through 4, as proposed by Selman and Selman, during childhood. Thus friendships begin as One-way Assistance, progress to Two-way Fair-Weather Cooperation, then to Intimate, Mutually Shared Relationships, and finally evolve into Autonomous Interdependent Friendships.

Key terms in this section:

sociogram	Two-way Fair Weather Cooperation
authoritarian leader	Intimate, Mutually Shared
democratic leader	Relationships
laissez faire leader	Autonomous Interdependent
One-way Assistance	Friendships

Self-Concept, Prejudice, and Sex Typing in Childhood

Probably the most important key to success and happiness in life
is a favorable self-image. According to Coopersmith, children's
self-image is influenced by four factors: significance, virtue,
competence and power. The higher an individual rates on all four
factors, the more favorable his or her self-concept. Self-concept
is also influenced by birth order, family size and warmth, school
achievement, ethnic group membership and, in a complex way,
socioeconomic standing.

The effect of prejudice on children is apparent as early as 2 years
of age. Both black and white children are biased in favor of
whites during the preschool years. This effect remains fairly constant for black children through the early school years, but for
whites it increases to the second grade and then decreases. Techniques for reducing racial prejudice include: increased positive
racial contact, vicarious interracial contact, reinforcement of
the color black, and perceptual differentiation.

Sex typing becomes more stable during the school years. Recent
evidence indicates that many students, especially older girls, are
becoming less stereotyped in their ideas of appropriate roles for
women. Such extra-familial influences as school and the media
influence sex typing.

Key terms in this section:

self-image (self-concept)	competence
significance	power
virtue	

The Child in the Family

Although the child spends a considerable amount of time with peers,
the family is still an important influence. Young children tend
to view their fathers as more punitive and dominating and less
nurturant than their mothers. By age 10, however, children usually
consider their same-sexed parent as more punitive. Media and
social class influence children's views of their parents.

Studies of one-parent families, of children of divorce, and of working mothers have generally indicated that so long as there is an atmosphere of love, support, and respect for family members there is an excellent prognosis for healthy development.

Emotional Disturbances in Childhood

The final section considers emotional problems of children. Such problems can be generally classified as behavior problems such as acting-out behavior and hyperactivity or hyperkinesis; as developmental disorders, including enuresis, encopresis, tics, and stuttering (stammering); as neurotic disorders, including anxiety neuroses, phobias, obsessive-compulsive neuroses, and neurotic-depressive conditions; or as psychotic disorders, such as early infantile autism and childhood schizophrenia.

Treatment of childhood emotional disorders varies from case to case and therapist to therapist. Placebo effects can mask the true effectiveness of treatments such as preventive therapy, supportive therapy, play therapy, child psychoanalysis, family therapy, behavior therapy, and drug therapy.

Key terms in this section:

behavior problems	neurotic depressive conditions
acting-out behavior	psychotic disorders
hyperactivity	early infantile autism
developmental disorders	childhood schizophrenia
enuresis	placebo effects
encopresis	preventive therapy
tics	supportive therapy
stuttering	play therapy
neurotic disorders	child psychoanalysis
anxiety neuroses	family therapy
phobias	behavior therapy
obsessive-compulsive neuroses	drug therapy

LEARNING OBJECTIVES

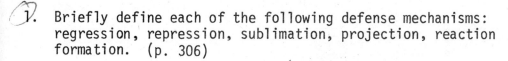

1. Briefly define each of the following defense mechanisms: regression, repression, sublimation, projection, reaction formation. (p. 306)

2. Explain Erikson's industry versus inferiority stage. (pp. 306-307)

3. Explain the statement, made by Opie and Opie, "Children have their own lore." (pp. 307-308)

4. Describe some functions that may be served by children's humor. (pp. 308-310)

5. Explain the functions that peer groups serve. (pp. 311-312)

6. Describe the use of sociograms in the study of peer groups. (p. 312)

7. Contrast the characteristics of popular and unpopular children. (pp. 312-313)

8. Briefly indicate the behavior of boys' clubs subjected to the following types of adult leadership. (pp. 313-314)

Authoritarian:

Laissez faire:

Democratic:

9. Compare and contrast American and Soviet children with respect to peer-group influences. (p. 314)

10. Trace the development of friendships during the childhood years. (pp. 315-317)

11. List and succinctly explain the four bases upon which people develop their self-images, according to Coopersmith. (p. 318)

a.

b.

c.

d.

12. Describe factors which have been found to influence children's self-concepts. (pp. 318-319)

13. Contrast the self-descriptions of black and white children. (pp. 319-320)

14. Describe four techniques used to reduce racial prejudice. (pp. 320-321)

a.

b.

c.

d.

15. Briefly describe the level of sex typing currently found among male and female schoolchildren. (pp. 321-322)

16. Summarize the views children have of same-sex and opposite-sex parents. (pp. 324-325)

17. Discuss the special problems of the one-parent family. (pp. 325-326)

18. Describe the impact that divorce has on parent-child inter-action. (pp. 327-328)

19. Tell why it is difficult to make generalizations about the effect working mothers' working has on their children. (pp. 328-330)

20. Describe the major categories of emotional disturbances suffered by school-aged children. (pp. 330-336)

21. Review major therapy techniques used to help children with emotional disorders. (pp. 336-338)

SELF TEST A

Circle the letter of the choice that completes each item.

1. Freud labeled the elementary school years the _____ period: (a) latency; (b) sexual; (c) industrious; (d) Oedipal.

2. If 8-year-old Steve proclaims very loudly and very frequently how very much he adores the new baby when he actually resents the attention being given to the newcomer instead of him, he would be using a defense mechanism called: (a) regression; (b) sublimation; (c) reaction formation; (d) projection.

3. According to Erikson, childhood is a period in which _____

is stressed. (a) sexuality; (b) industry; (c) autonomy; (d) peer-group status.

4. Which of the following is <u>not</u> a function served by children's humor? (a) It helps children <u>deal</u> with sexuality. (b) It helps children deal with gender permanence. (c) It helps relieve anxiety. (d) It provides information about the world.

5. Peer-group pressure has the greatest influence on a child's judgments when the: (a) child's status in the group is high; (b) child is an adolescent; (c) material to be evaluated is ambiguous; (d) material to be evaluated is familiar.

6. Bob is a very popular child in his classroom. We would <u>not</u> expect Bob to: (a) be healthy; (b) have very high self-esteem; (c) be able to initiate actions; (d) be physically attractive.

7. Lewin, Lippit, and White (1939) found that children were more friendly and more apt to work when the leader left the room when that leader who was one was: (a) authoritarian; (b) laissez faire; (c) democratic; (d) a peer.

8. Coopersmith reports that by age 12 children's friendships begin to be: (a) autonomous, independent; (b) one-way assistance; (c) two-way fair-weather cooperation; (d) less important.

9. Coopersmith (1967) concluded that people develop their self-concepts according to four bases: (a) significance, competence, virtue, and power; (b) power, physical attractiveness, age, and competence; (c) competence, power, size, and intellectual abilities; (d) productivity, power, intellectual ability, and virtue.

10. Children are more likely to get into trouble if they are from a home that is: (a) broken by death; (b) broken by divorce; (c) disrupted by argument, anger, or failure; (d) a two-paycheck home.

PRACTICE EXERCISES

<u>Completion</u>

Supply the words or phrases that best complete these sentences.

1. Freud termed the elementary school years the _____ period, considering it an island of relative sexual quiescence between the turbulent preschool years and the storminess of adolescence.

2. During trying times, children often _____, showing behavior of an earlier age, attempting to recapture remembered security.

3. According to Erikson, school age is the age when

   _____ becomes important. No longer are children content to play; they must become workers.

4. Sixth-graders who are rated as more "_____-oriented" report engaging in more antisocial behavior than do

   "_____-oriented" children.

5. Popular children tend to be healthy, vigorous, well poised,

   and capable of initiative, but they are also _____

   and _____.

6. Lewin, Lippitt, and White (1939) set up several clubs of 10-year-old boys, run in turn by authoritarian, democratic, and laissez-faire leaders. Under authoritarian leadership, there was either a high level of aggression or a high level of

   _____, which quickly gave way to _____ when the leader left the room.

7. Probably the most important key to success and happiness in

   life is a favorable _____-_____.

8. According to Sheikh and Beglis (1973), black children described

   themselves more often in terms of basic _____

   and less often in terms of _____ and

   _____.

9. A recent survey of 1600 fourth-, sixth-, eighth, and tenth-grade suburban students revealed some decidedly stereotyped ways of thinking. But it also showed that many students,

   especially _____ _____, express a willing-ness to "grant women greater participation in the social, economic, and political spheres."

10. Young children tend to fear their _____ more than

    their _____ and to see their _____ as more punitive, more dominating, and less nurturant (Kagan and Lemkin 1960; Kagan 1956); but children over age 10 usually

    consider their _____-_____ parent as the most

punitive.

True-False

Circle T if the statement is true, F if the statement is false.

T F 1. Freud's conceptualization of childhood as a latency period is not correct.

T F 2. Children often use humor to help relieve anxiety they have.

T F 3. Peer groups' values always conflict with those of parents.

T F 4. Popular children generally have the highest level of self-esteem in their groups.

T F 5. Friendships in childhood generally become more mutual and autonomous.

T F 6. Self-concept is thought to be affected, in part, by a person's perception of how much other people love them, and this is called significance.

T F 7. Children in minorities and from lower socioeconomic strata always have lower self-esteem.

T F 8. Children over 10 years of age generally view their same-sexed parent as more punitive.

T F 9. Studies indicate that divorced parents often communicate less well with their children than do nondivorced parents.

T F 10. A mother's working has advantages but always has a deleterious effect on children.

Word Scramble

Unscramble the 10 items. Then arrange the circled letters to complete the sentence below.

1.

G S I O R E S R E N

Acting younger than one's years as a defense mechanism

2.

F R I Y N T I O E I R

Negative outcome of Eriksonian crises of childhood

139

3. _ _ _O_ _ _ _O

O C G M A S I O R

Tool for examining peer-group popularity

4. _ _ _O_ _

R E V I U T

Gives high self-esteem by attaining ethical and moral
standards

5. _ _ _O_O_ _ _

I S C O V U I R A

Interracial contact via a story

6. _ _O_ _ _ _ _

U I S E N S E R

Bedwetting

7. O_ _ _ _ _ _

I E T N A X Y

Type of childhood neurosis characterized by extreme shyness,
clinging, and psychosomatic complaints

8. _ _ _ _ _ _ _ _O_ _ _

P I R I H E S S K E N Y

Syndrome of extreme distractibility, agitation, and poor
impulse control

9. _ _ _ _ _ _O_ _ _

R E U P T I S V O P

Therapy in which child expresses concerns

10. _O_ _ _ _ _

L B O P C E A

Substance that helps but has no actual therapeutic value

A psychosis that occurs early in life and results in the
child being "cutoff" from others is called early

_ _ _ _ _ _ _ _ _ _ _ _ _ _ _.

SELF TEST B

Circle the letter of the choice that completes each item.

1. Mary has been told "no cookies before dinner," but she very much wants one of the cookies she sees on the plate in her kitchen. She wants one so badly she must close her eyes so she cannot see them to keep from taking one. Mary is using: (a) regression; (b) repression; (c) sublimation; (d) projection.

2. One of the defense mechanisms used in middle childhood is sublimation, through which children: (a) block their true feelings; (b) attribute their unacceptable thoughts and motives to others; (c) channel their sexual energy into such acceptable activities as sports; (d) say things which are opposite to how they actually feel.

3. Children's lore, which they hand down to one another, is: (a) always original; (b) rarely imitative; (c) rarely original; (d) a recent phenomenon.

4. To assess popularity among children, researchers use a technique called a: (a) pictogram; (b) sociogram; (c) reaction formation; (d) holograph.

5. Bronfenbrenner (1967) found in his study of Russian and American 12-year-olds that peer-group pressures: (a) influenced Russian children toward adult standards and American children away from adult standards; (b) influenced Russian children away from adult standards and American children toward adult standards; (c) were the same for children in both groups; (d) were very strong for American children but had little effect upon the behavior of Russian children.

6. Two recent studies showed that, in comparison to middle-class children, minority-group children had: (a) lower self-esteem; (b) less self-confidence; (c) higher self-esteem; (d) unclear self-images.

7. Among children over the age of 10, the most punitive parent is usually considered to be the: (a) opposite-sex parent; (b) same-sex parent; (c) father; (d) mother.

8. Decreasing racial prejudice can be accomplished by constructing interracial teams that work on puzzles and receive praise for their work. This is an example of a technique called: (a) increased positive racial contact; (b) vicarious interracial contact; (c) reinforcement of the color black; (d) perceptual differentiation.

9. Tommy just cannot sit still. He often jumps up and runs around the classroom and cannot concentrate on a task for even moderately

long periods of time. Tommy probably has: (a) enuresis; (b) encopresis; (c) hyperactivity; (d) anxiety neurosis.

10. In therapy, the psychologist lets Frances talk about whatever is bothering her at home or school. The therapist is warm and understanding and tries to help Frances cope. This therapy is: (a) childhood psychoanalysis; (b) supportive therapy; (c) preventive therapy; (d) play therapy.

VIGNETTES

1. Harold is an unpopular child. If you were to intervene to attempt to make him more popular, what would you include in your treatment?

2. Mrs. Smith is expecting her first child in four months. She has been working for four years at a job quite satisfying. She asks you whether she should continue to work after her child is born. What advice would you give?

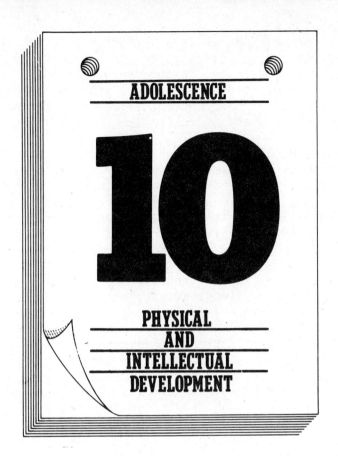

ADOLESCENCE

10

PHYSICAL
AND
INTELLECTUAL
DEVELOPMENT

INTEGRATOR

Chapter 10 will consider the physical development of adolescence.
Not since the infancy stage, considered in Chapter 3, will physical
change in the person be so rapid and pronounced--adolescence mark-
ing the attainment of adult physical stature. The importance of
this physical growth has clear implications for the personality and
social development of the adolescent and for the adult as well.
Chapters 4, 6, and 8 traced intellectual development as conceived
by Piaget. In Chapter 10, this theoretical orientation is continued as we look at adolescence as a period of formal operational
thinking, the culmination of intellectual development. More-mature
moral reasoning and consideration of vocational choices are discussed as additional developments that relate to adolescent cognitive functioning.

OVERVIEW

Adolescence: Definition and Physiological Changes

Adolescence is a period of transition between childhood and adulthood. It begins with pubescence, a stage of rapid physiological
growth and sexual maturation, which lasts about two years. It ends

with puberty, the point at which a person is able to reproduce. Unlike some primitive societies which use a preordained age or menarche to signal adulthood, Western societies do not provide a clear cut end of adolescence. In recent years a new stage of development, youth, has been conceptualized as a period of transition between adulthood and adolescence.

Dramatic physiological changes mark adolescence. Maturation during pubescence includes development of primary and secondary sex characteristics as well as the sudden height increase of the adolescent growth spurt. The trend toward earlier growth and maturation of each generation is called the secular trend. This trend, which has now leveled off, is probably due to numerous factors including improved nutrition and health care and the bicycle effect.

The physical manifestations of adolescence include a sharp increase in height which affects almost all skeletal and muscular dimensions. The secondary sex characteristics become apparent as well. These include the appearance of axillary and pubic hair in both sexes and facial hair for boys. Breast development with enlargement of the nipples and areolas and the onset of menstruation are important developments for girls. Boys may begin to experience nocturnal emissions. Adolescents may experience such skin changes as acne, which is related to androgen levels, at this time.

The adolescent's rapid body changes affect self-concept and personality; teenagers are more concerned about their physical appearance than about any other aspect of themselves. The effect of early or late maturing is of particular importance, although any effect of this variable seems to disappear by adulthood. Anorexia nervosa, a prolonged and severe refusal to eat, is a disorder afflicting predominantly adolescent girls.

Key terms in this section:

pubescence	bicycle effect
puberty	axillary hair
menarche	areola
youth	menstruation
primary sex characteristics	nocturnal emission
secondary sex characteristics	acne
adolescent growth spurt	androgen
secular trend	anorexia nervosa

Intellectual Development in Adolescence

The adolescent years correspond to Piaget's final cognitive stage, formal operations. The individual now develops the ability to think abstractly and can use hypothetico-deductive reasoning. The pendulum problem is often used to demonstrate these skills and the increased flexibility characterizing adolescent thought. Adolescents do exhibit egocentrism to a degree as is evidenced by the imaginary audience and personal fable, but it is quite different from the egocentrism of childhood. The advancing cognitive development makes it possible for adolescents to attain higher levels of moral reasoning. Moral development is possible but not guaranteed.

Making a vocational choice is a major challenge for adolescents. An individual's choice is affected by socioeconomic status, parents, school experiences and personality factors. For many young adults, intellectual development is affected by the college experience. There are sex differences in development at this time, with females being more inhibited and having lower self-esteem than males. Lack of female role models and fear of success have been cited as possible causes of these differences. College "dropouts" vary in personality and in reasons for leaving school. The decision to leave is often a positive step. The concept of youth implies a transitional period between adolescence and adulthood.

Key terms in this section:

formal operations	imaginary audience
hypothetico-deductive reasoning	personal fable
pendulum problem	fear of success

LEARNING OBJECTIVES

1. Explain what is meant by the term "adolescence." (p. 344)

2. Differentiate between adolescence and youth. (p. 364)

3. Describe the "secular trend" in growth and maturation and tell why it occurs. (pp. 345-346)

4. Describe the physical changes that occur during the adolescent growth spurt. (pp. 346-347)

5. Briefly discuss the variables involved in the impact of menstruation on adolescent girls. (pp. 347-348)

6. Tell how physical development can affect personality development in adolescence. (pp. 348-350)

7. Discuss the causes and treatment of anorexia nervosa. (pp. 350-351)

8. Describe the major features of thought during the formal operations period. (p. 352)

9. Describe the pendulum problem and explain how it is used to study adolescent thought. (pp. 352-353)

10. Briefly describe adolescent moral development. (pp. 355-357)

11. Briefly explain "imaginary audience" and "personal fable."
    (p. 354)

12. Tell how the adolescent eventually overcomes his egocentrism.
    (p. 355)

13. Explain how the college experience can influence intellectual development. (pp. 359-362)

14. Discuss the factors that can influence vocational development. (pp. 357-359)

15. Explain why there is no one "dropout personality." (pp. 362-364)

SELF TEST A

Circle the letter of the choice that completes each item.

1. In Western society, adolescence is considered to end at: (a) age 18; (b) age 19; (c) the late teens or early 20's; (d) age 21.

2. The stage of rapid physiological growth, when reproductive functions and primary sex organs mature, is called: (a) pubescence; (b) puberty; (c) adolescence; (d) youth.

3. The secular trend describes the: (a) movement away from religion by today's teens; (b) trend over the centuries toward large-size and earlier maturation; (c) worldwide trend toward healthier, better-nourished children; (d) trend toward sexual activity in adolescents.

4. Most males attain adult height by age: (a) 18; (b) 21; (c) 17; (d) 23.

5. Adolescent self-concepts depend largely on: (a) how attractive young people consider themselves; (b) sexual maturity; (c) birth order and family size; (d) socioeconomic status.

6. In a study comparing early- and late-maturing boys, Mussen and Jones (1957) found that: (a) early maturers were more aggressive; (b) late maturers felt more adequate and were more cooperative with their parents; (c) early maturers were more self-confident and independent; (d) the effects of late maturation lasted far into adulthood.

7. Sally is 16 years old. She refuses to eat and thus weighs only 87 pounds; she is 5 feet 5 inches tall. She has lost 30 pounds in three months. She would most likely be diagnosed as having: (a) anxiety neurosis; (b) menarche; (c) dietary dysfunction; (d) anorexia nervosa.

8. According to Piaget, by age 16: (a) the libido is reawakened and threatens the id-ego balance; (b) a person's way of thinking is almost fully formed; (c) egocentrism diminishes; (d) abstract thought declines.

9. Generally, when compared to people from the middle and higher social classes, people from the lower social classes have: (a) a higher vocational goal; (b) a lower vocational goal; (c) about the same aspirations for their vocational development; (d) vacillating aspirations which change rapidly until their late 20's.

10. Women at college do not seem to have the same type of experiences as do men. Research indicates that this may be an underlying cause of: (a) higher self-esteem in women; (b) less inhibition in women; (c) lower self-esteem in women; (d) lower grades for women.

PRACTICE EXERCISES

Completion

Supply the words or phrases that best complete these sentences.

1. _____ lasts about two years and ends in

   _____, the point at which an individual is sexually mature and able to reproduce.

2. In many contemporary primitive societies, children move abruptly into adulthood at some preordained age, or at _____

   _____, the advent of menstruation.

3. At puberty, maturation of the reproductive organs is accom-

   plished by an ___adolescent___ ___growth___

   ___spurt___.

4. The trend toward larger size and earlier maturation is known

   as the ___secular___ trend, since it has been observed from one century to another.

5. The activity of the _____ glands is often responsible for acne in adolescents.

6. Most young teenagers are more concerned about their

   _____ _____ than about any other aspect of themselves.

7. In a study of 17-year-old boys, Mussen and Jones (1957) found

   that _____ maturers showed self-confidence, independence, and the ability to play an adult role in interpersonal rela-

   tionships and that although _____-maturing boys try harder to be accepted socially, their attempts are often child-ish and affected.

8. A prolonged and severe refusal to eat, often resulting in

   death, is called _____ _____.

9. According to Piaget, by about the age of __16__, a per-son's way of thinking is almost formed. There are no more

   qualitative leaps.

10. A counterpart to the imaginary audience, the _personal_

    fable, is the adolescent's belief that he is special because so many people are interested in him.

Matching

In the blank to the left of each definition, write the letter that indicates the term defined.

_____ 1. Period of rapid physiological change

_b_ 2. Point of reproductive capability

_h_ 3. Transition from adolescence to adulthood

_a_ 4. Increasing genetic diversity yielding a secular trend

_e_ 5. Dark area around breast nipple

_g_ 6. Hormones possibly related to acne

_i_ 7. Used to assess adolescent cognition

_c_ 8. Belief that others are "watching"--held by adolescents

_d_ 9. Belief that the adolescent is too special for subjection to rules governing others

_f_

10. Contribute to college women's lower self-esteem

a. bicycle effect
b. puberty
c. imaginary audience
d. personal fable
e. areola

f. fear of success
g. androgens
h. youth
i. pubescence
j. pendulum problem

True-False

Circle T if the statement is true, F if the statement is false.

T (F) 1. Adolescents experience rapid physiological change during the period of puberty.

(T) F 2. The timing of physical development is of importance for adolescent personality development.

T (F) 3. The secular trend is continuing into the 1980s.

(T) F 4. Most adolescent girls reach adult height at age 18, while males generally do so by 21.

T (F) 5. Climate greatly affects the onset of menstruation.

T (F) 6. Being forewarned and prepared has little effect on a girls' reaction to menarche.

T (F) 7. Anorexia nervosa seldom requires professional care.

(T) F 8. Adolescents exhibit adultlike hypothesis-testing skills.

T (F) 9. Vocational choice is usually made independent of past schooling experiences.

(T) F 10. There is a wide variety of reasons why people leave college, but it is usually a positive step.

SELF TEST B

Circle the letter of the choice that completes each item.

1. The end of pubescence is marked by: (a) parenthood; (b) legal adulthood; (c) puberty; (d) the adolescent growth spurt.

2. Menarche is the: (a) beginning of menstruation; (b) period when reproductive functions and primary sex organs mature; (c) point at which an individual is sexually mature; (d) point at which nocturnal emissions begin.

3. Which of the following statements, according to Keniston, is not true of the youth culture? (a) It emphasizes disengagement from adult values. (b) It is belligerently nonadult. (c) It is

explicitly antiadult. (d) It is restricted to the American culture.

4. Harold is developing secondary sex characteristics. Which of the following is <u>not</u> one of these characteristics? (a) development of axillary hair; (b) development of pubic hair; (c) breast enlargement; (d) production of sperm.

5. Boys and girls in adolescence develop acne because of: (a) increased activity of the sebaceous glands; (b) increased activity of the sex glands; (c) the development of the areolas; (d) their diet being poor.

6. Which of the following does <u>not</u> have an effect on the onset of menstruation? (a) climate; (b) urban versus rural life; (c) genetics; (d) nutrition.

7. Piaget terms the adolescent years the stage of: (a) formal operations; (b) egocentrism; (d) identity; (d) crises.

8. In order to understand universal moral principles, people have to be: (a) capable of abstract reasoning; (b) brought up in a religious home; (c) sexually mature; (d) in concrete operations.

9. Kohlberg believes that people: (a) cannot be taught to elevate their moral thinking; (b) can be taught to elevate their moral thinking; (c) are born with certain predispositions toward moral judgments; (d) achieve their terminal level of moral reasoning during pubescence.

10. Research has shown that intellectual development: (a) begins at adolescence; (b) ends at adolescence; (c) continues after adolescence; (d) reverses and begins to decline after adolescence.

VIGNETTES

1. Mary is pregnant. She is 15 years old and her explanation for not using birth control is that she didn't believe that it could happen to her. Her parents are thunderstruck by this statement since they have thoroughly explained the "facts of life" to her. How might you explain Mary's explanation?

2. You are working as a high school "job day" counselor. What factors would you expect to influence the vocational choices of your students? What would you stress in helping the students?

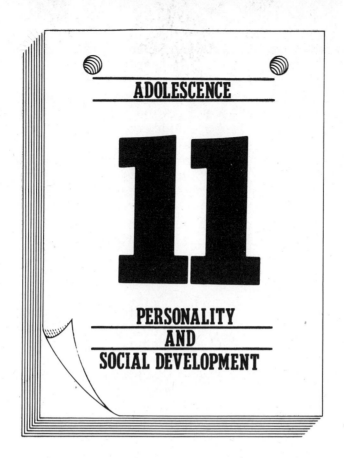

ADOLESCENCE

11

PERSONALITY
AND
SOCIAL DEVELOPMENT

INTEGRATOR

Chapter 11 extends the discussion of personality and social development begun in Chapter 5 and continued in Chapters 7 and 9. We have
seen that up to the end of adolescence the individual begins to
develop true friendships, becomes more autonomous from his parents,
and reaches physical maturation. The relationship of adolescents
to parents and peers and the impact of sexual maturation will thus
be central issues in this chapter. The solving of problems facing
the adolescent is important for his entry into adulthood; thus,
just as adolescence bridges childhood and adulthood, Chapter 11
represents a bridge between the earlier chapters of the text and
the remaining material.

OVERVIEW

Theoretical Perspectives and the Search for Identity

The chapter begins by considering several theoretical views of
adolescence. G. Stanley Hall, for example, saw adolescence as a
period of "storm and stress" marked by vacillating and contradicting
emotions. Margaret Mead, on the other hand, claimed that adolescence
may be smooth or stressful, depending on cultural factors. Albert

Bandura maintains that adolescence, even in America, is not as stressful as Hall thought. Data gathered by Offer and Offer, in which adolescents were classified as exhibiting continuous growth, surgent growth, or tumultuous growth support Bandura's view. The Freuds considered the adolescent period as a genital stage in which libido is reawakened and basic conflicts are resolved. Intellectualization and asceticism are defense mechanisms frequently employed by adolescents to avoid being overwhelmed by these conflicts. Finally, according to Erikson, adolescence is when the crises of identity versus role confusion must be resolved. The search for identity is probably the most important task for the adolescent. According to Marcia, in developing a sense of self adolescents can be classified as exhibiting identity achievement, foreclosure, identity diffusion and moratorium.

Key terms in this section:

continuous growth	asceticism
surgent growth	identity vs. role confusion
tumultuous growth	identity achievement
libido	foreclosure
genital stage	identity diffusion
intellectualization	moratorium

Relationships with Parents and Peers

Becoming independent is another major aspect of adolescence. Although the relationship between parents and teenagers is not always smooth, it is generally marked by mutual positive regard. Teens often are ambivalent about their dependence on parents and their desire for independence.

While the peer group is not all powerful, it does exert a major influence on the typical teenager. Teens identify with other teens rather than with people of their own race, religion, community or sex. The views of peers seem more important for problems with immediate consequences, but for more long ranged decisions teens tend to rely more on parents.

Many teens are caught up in generational chauvinism which is furthered by society's emphasis on youth.

Friendships become vitally important during adolescence. Friendships, based upon the five dimensions of similarity, reciprocity, compatibility, structure and role-modeling, continue their importance with some changes in patterns throughout the life span.

Key terms in this section:

generational chauvinism	compatibility
similarity	structure
reciprocity	role-modeling

Sexuality

Adolescent sexual activity is tied to young people's self-image and developing identity. Parents today are in a state of transition; and although many conflicts between parents and adolescent children focus on sexuality, parents today tend to be more liberal and less punitive than in generations past. When parents and children do discuss sex, their conversations tend to be abstract rather than particular.

Recent surveys have indicated that adolescent sexual activity is increasing, especially among females of all educational backgrounds. Among sexually active teens, however, promiscuity is not the norm. The tendency is to enter into meaningful, monogamous relationships rather than promiscuous ones.

Change is even more evident in attitudes toward sexuality than in sexual behavior. Current attitudes are more liberal; most males do not lose respect for females who have intercourse prior to marriage and most members of both sexes approve of living together prior to marriage. Male adolescents are more sexually active than females; however, it is unclear whether this is because of biological or cultural factors.

Homosexuality is more visible in American society today. Acceptance of homosexuality has increased but many adolescents as well as adults maintain negative or ambivalent feelings about homosexual preferences.

Problems of Adolescence

The next several sections deal with problems of adolescence. Sexually related problems include venereal disease and pregnancy. The incidence of both during the adolescent period is on the incline. These problems seem related to adolescent egocentrism and the personal fable as well as other factors. The consequences of adolescent parenthood are wide ranging for society as a whole as well as the adolescents themselves who have special needs.

Dropping out of school is another problem which is considered, although fewer adolescents drop out now than did in the 1950s. The tight job market and the increasing technology of American society have made staying in school even more important today.

Poor black students are most likely to drop out of school. Although it is impossible to delineate the precise reasons for dropping out, adolescents who leave school tend to fall into the involuntary dropout, retarded dropout, or capable dropout class.

Drug abuse continues as a problem during adolescence as well as adulthood. In general, youthful drug-taking patterns tend to follow those of the adult society with alcohol and marijuana being commonly abused drugs. Tobacco use is also on the rise in teenage populations despite the health risks clearly involved.

Juvenile delinquency is the last problem considered. Delinquency may involve two types of cases, the status offender or the criminal offender. Although boys are more likely to be arrested than girls, the crime rate among girls is rising. The incidence of delinquency is related to social background, school experience, home atmosphere, and the adolescent's personality. Delinquents have been classified as impulsive, narcissistic, emotionally empty, or depressed.

Despite the challenges and problems of adolescence, teenagers typically have many ego strengths. The numerous positive aspects of adolescence listed in Table 11-3 attest to the fact that adolescents have many positive attributes that they too frequently fail to recognize and value.

Key terms in this section:

involuntary dropout   narcissistic delinquent
retarded dropout   emotionally empty delinquent
capable dropout   depressed delinquent
status offender   ego strengths
impulsive delinquent

LEARNING OBJECTIVES

1. Briefly summarize the views of adolescence held by the fol-
    lowing: (pp. 370-372)

    G. Stanley Hall

    Margaret Mead

    Albert Bandura

Sigmund Freud

Anna Freud

Erik Erikson

2. Review the findings of Offer and Offer regarding adolescent
   turmoil. (p. 370)

3. List and explain Marcia's four categories of identity status.
   (pp. 372-373)

   a.

   b.

   c.

d.

4. Describe, in general, the relationship between the typical adolescent and his or her parents. (p. 374)

5. Describe the relative influences of parents versus peers on adolescents' decisions. (p. 376)

6. Explain what is meant by the term "generational chauvinism." (p. 377)

7. List five dimensions of friendship for the adolescent. (p. 378)

   a.

   b.

   c.

d.

e.

8. Discuss the factors that are bound up in adolescent sexuality.
    (pp. 379-380)

9. Briefly discuss the changes in sexual practices that have
    occurred in recent years among adolescents. (pp. 381-382)

10. Describe the changes in attitudes that have accompanied the
    changes in behavior described above. (pp. 383-384)

11. Discuss the bases of sex differences in sexual responses in
    adolescents. (pp. 384-385)

12. Describe the possible causes of increases in pregnancy and venereal disease in adolescent populations. (pp. 386-387, 388-390)

13. Explain the consequences of teenage parenthood for society and the teenagers involved. (pp. 387-388)

14. Discuss the effect of dropping out of school on the vocational and social development of the individual. (pp. 390-391)

15. List the variables that have been found to be associated with dropping out of school. (pp. 391-392)

16. List and describe three types of adolescent dropouts. (p. 391)

    a.

b.

c.

17. Briefly summarize the data on patterns of drug use among teen-
    agers. (pp. 392-395)

18. Differentiate between the status offender and the criminal
    delinquent. (p. 395)

19. List and describe four types of juvenile delinquent. (p. 397)

    a.

    b.

    c.

d.

20. Describe some major factors associated with criminal delin-
     quency in adolescents. (pp. 396-397)

21. Describe the ego strengths of adolescents. (pp. 397-400)

SELF TEST A

Circle the letter of the choice that completes each item.

1. Adolescence was characterized as Sturm and Drang (storm and
stress) by: (a) Mead; (b) Hall; (c) Bandura; (d) Freud.

2. Offer and Offer found that about 20 percent of the adolescents
they interviewed exhibited: (a) a moratorium on growth; (b) surgent
growth; (c) continuous growth; (d) tumultuous growth.

3. Sharon plans to be a teacher. She has always been told that
she is very good with children. Both of her parents are teachers
and Sharon has never really questioned their desire that she too
should teach. According to Marcia, Sharon's identity status is
one of: (a) achievement; (b) diffusion; (c) moratorium; (d) foreclosure.

4. Sigmund Freud considered the keynote of adolescence to be:
(a) the latency period of sexual growth; (b) the genital stage of
mature sexuality; (c) the growth of character; (d) achievement of
identity.

5. Sorensen (1973) found that teenagers are most likely to identify
with: (a) other teenagers; (b) people of their own race; (c) people
of their own sex; (d) people of their community.

6. The percentage of women in their late teens and mid-20's who
have had sexual intercourse has _____ since Kinsey's (1953) figures. (a) stayed about the same; (b) doubled; (c) quadrupled;
(d) declined.

7. A significant majority of teenagers think that it is immoral:
(a) for unmarried persons to have sex; (b) for a boy to force a
girl into sex; (c) to have sex without love; (d) to live together
before marriage.

8. The favorite teenage alcoholic drink is: (a) beer; (b) wine;
(c) whiskey; (d) vodka.

9. The typical delinquent is a: (a) girl of 15 who lives with one
parent and several siblings; (b) glack ghetto youth of 16; (c) boy
of 15 who lives with one parent and several siblings; (d) boy or
girl from a middle-class urban setting.

10. The major reason why sexually active teenage girls do not use
contraceptives is that they: (a) think that they cannot become
pregnant; (b) cannot obtain contraceptives; (c) do not approve of
contraceptives; (d) feel that it is their boyfriends' responsibility.

PRACTICE EXERCISES

Completion

Supply the words or phrases that best complete these sentences.

1. G. Stanley Hall saw adolescence as a period of storm and

    stress, a period of ____contradictory____ and ____vacillating____
    emotions.

2. Sigmund Freud considered the ____genital____ ____stage____
    of mature sexuality the keynote of adolescence.

3. Erik Erikson identified adolescence as a crisis of

    ____identity____ versus ____role____ ____confusion____ .

4. A recent study found that parents are troubled by many facets
    of teenage life, but they are generally positive about the
    young people themselves. Sorensen (1973) found that most teen-

    agers say they really ____know____ , ____like____ , and

163

_____respect_____ their parents.

5. Teenagers tend to hold the __same__ political and religious attitudes as their parents.

6. When parents and children discuss sex, conversations are

    usually __general__ rather than __specific__.

7. Reasons for leaving school are many. Voss, Wendling, and

    Elliott (1966) set up three categories: the __involuntary__ dropout, who must leave school because of physical disability

    or family emergency; the __retarded__ __incapable__ dropout, who is in-

    capable of doing high school work; and the __capable__ dropout, who has the ability to graduate.

8. The __status__ __offender__ is the young person who has been truant, run away from home, or done something else that is ordinarily not considered criminal except when com- mitted by a minor.

9. The picture of the delinquent's family that emerges from study

    after study is one of parents who are __hostile__ or

    __indifferent__ but rarely __affectionate__.

10. The most striking changes in sexual matters, overall, have

    been among __women__ of all educational levels.

True-False

Circle T if the statement is true, F if the statement is false.

(T) F   1. Data support the idea of Hall that adolescence is always a period of storm and stress.

(T) F   2. A "playboy" type who actively avoids commitment to goals is classified as identity diffuse.

(T) F   3. Conflicts between parents and adolescents usually reflect differing opinions about timing rather than issues.

T (F)   4. The attitudes of adolescents today regarding sex have changed compared to earlier generations, but their sex- ual behavior has not.

(T) F   5. Adolescents today are more promiscuous than in times past.

164

Ⓣ F   6.   Most adolescents view homosexuality as normal though they themselves would not participate in a homosexual relationship.

Ⓣ F   7.   Teenage pregnancies face greater risk of complications than when the mother is in her 20's.

Ⓣ F   8.   Nonavailability of contraceptives and the personal fable are two major reasons that adolescents seldom practice birth control.

Ⓣ F   9.   Most adolescents who leave school are either incapable of doing the work or are forced to leave by financial pressures.

T Ⓕ 10.   The use of drugs has declined steadily since 1975 in American adolescent populations.

Word Scrambler

Unscramble the ten items. Then arrange the circled letters to complete the sentence below.

1. L I B Ⓘ D O
   I L I D O B
   Sexual energy

2. G E Ⓝ I T A L
   E A T L G I N
   The stage of adolescence, according to Freud

3. _ _ _ _ _ _ _ _ _ _ _ _ Ⓤ _
   A E L I M E S T I N C L T U L
   Ego defense based upon abstract thought   *Intellectualism*

4. _ _ _ _ _ _ Ⓘ _ _ _
   C S C M A I E I T S
   Ego defense using self-denial   *asceticism*

5. _ _ Ⓔ _ Ⓔ _ _ _ _ _
   I V E E N A E C M H T
   Knowing oneself after crisis of searching in this type of identity   *achievement*

6. _ _ _ _ _ _ _ Ⓞ _ _ _
   E R O U C F L O S R E
   Identity based on accepting other's plans   *foreclosure*

7. O _ _ _ _ _ _ _ _ _
   R I O R O M U T M A *moratorium*

Identity period of questioning and searching

8. _ O _ _ _ _ _ _
   A B A E C P L *Capable*

Dropout who has ability

9. _ _ _ O _ _ _ _ _ _ _
   M Y I A R I S L I T *similarit*

Basis of friendship stemming from shared values

Adolescents often reject other generations and hold the view that they themselves do everything better. This is known as generational C H A U V A N I S m.

SELF TEST B

Circle the letter of the choice that completes each item.

1. The prime danger at adolescence, according to Erikson, is:
(a) homosexuality; (b) identity confusion; (c) intellectualization;
(d) cognitive dissonance.

2. Fourteen-year-old Bill deals with his strong sexual urges by refusing to date and convincing himself that he is not interested in girls. Bill is using the defense mechanism called: (a) projection; (b) sublimation; (c) intellectualization; (d) asceticism.

3. The defense mechanism by which perceptions are translated into abstract thought is called: (a) libido; (b) asceticism; (c) intellectualization; (d) regression.

4. Alice is trying to decide whether to go to college. She is most likely to seek advice from: (a) no one; (b) her peer group; (c) her best friend; (d) her parents.

5. Which of the following is not a dimension of friendship?
(a) age; (b) similarity; (c) structure; (d) role modeling.

6. Venereal disease among teenagers: (a) is very rare; (b) has increased in recent years; (c) has declined in recent years; (d) is primarily the result of increased promiscuity in recent years.

7. Which of the following is not listed as a consequence of

166

teenage pregnancy? (a) complications in pregnancy; (b) problems in child rearing; (c) restricted life experiences; (d) increased marriage stability.

8. "I just didn't believe I could get pregnant." This statement reflects one cause of teenage pregnancy, the: (a) availability of contraceptives; (b) personal fable; (c) embarrassment over sexual matters; (d) fear of parent's finding contraceptives.

9. The most heavily abused and frequently used drug in the United States is: (a) alcohol; (b) marijuana; (c) tobacco; (d) LSD.

10. Students who are less likely to smoke marijuana are those who: (a) are most strongly oriented toward achievement; (b) come from middle and upper classes; (c) drink heavily; (d) drop out of school.

VIGNETTES

1. If you were invited to address a group of parents of adolescents on the topic of "communication with your teenager," what major points would you want to get across?

2. Several of your classmates are having a "bull session" on the topic of sex education. One point of view is that sex education should be conducted by parents, not schools. How might you respond if you wanted to shift the focus from who should do it to what they should do?

YOUNG
ADULTHOOD

12

PHYSICAL
AND
INTELLECTUAL
DEVELOPMENT

INTEGRATOR

The adolescent growth spurt described in Chapter 10 has stabilized by young adulthood and, as Chapters 12 and 14 will show, physical development remains fairly stable until old age, considered in Chapter 16, when some decline is noticed. The degree of decline will be greatly affected by the type of health regimen followed in the early-adulthood years.

Similarly, intellectual development remains fairly stable during adulthood. The moral development of adults differs from that of adolescents in that adult development is influenced more by personal life experiences than by instruction.

The changing aspects of career development described in this chapter have some consequences for the social and personality development of the young adult, described in Chapter 13. In particular, as more women pursue their career goals and dual-career families become more popular, the nature of parenthood will probably also change.

OVERVIEW

Physical Development of Young Adults

Physical development in adults between 20 and 40 years of age is characterized by strength, energy, and endurance. Most of the body systems are functioning at their best at this time, with only slight decline in such things as manual dexterity and hearing. Young adults are also generally healthier than any other segment of the population. Before the age of 35, the leading cause of death is accidents, while after this age, diseases tend to become more important causes. The implications of higher incidences of violent deaths among men than women are considered. Several factors, including lifestyle, education. gender. marital status, and life stress, are related to health status. For women, hormonal fluctuations associated with ovulation and menstruation can have clear effects on their behavior. Cultural as well as physiological factors may contribute to cyclical shifts in the moods of women and, possibly, men.

Intellectual Functioning of Young Adults

Not only are young adults at the peak of physical development, but their intellectual functioning is at a high level as well. This section considers changes in thought processes that occur at this time. An important distinction is made between fluid and crystallized intelligence, the former involving conceptual and abstract reasoning, and the latter involving tasks that are more dependent on education and cultural background. Performance tends to decline on the first kind of task but improve on the second.

Piagetian-based tasks indicate that, with the exceptions of conservation of volume and transitivity, young adults function at a higher level than both younger- and older-aged groups. Animistic responses are more frequent in this age group than would be expected from the Piagetian viewpoint.

The moral development of adults seems to be affected by life experiences, particularly for those adults with strong emotional impact. Fully principled thinking (Kohlberg's stages 5 and 6), if attained, is usually done so in the late 20's. Kohlberg maintains that cognitive growth sets the upper limit of moral development but attainment of that limit rests upon personal experiences. Women's moral development may be greatly affected by cultural sex-role models. Gilligan has postulated a separate sequence of moral development for women which includes: orientation of individual survival, goodness as self-sacrifice, and morality of nonviolence, with transitions between each level.

While intellectual functioning, moral reasoning, and physical well-being are at their peak during the 20's, creativity may not be a

169

hallmark of the young adulthood period.

Key terms in this section:

fluid vs. crystallized
    intelligence
transitivity
orientation of individual
    survival

goodness as self-sacrifice
morality of nonviolence
moral transitions
creativity

Career Development

The last section considers the factors that are involved in one's
choice of a career. The importance of the critical event in vocational selection is considered. Although many elements play a
role in one's choice of vocation and job satisfaction, the sex of
the individual is one of the most influential. Traditional bar-
riers and fear of success are considered as contributing to male-
female vocational differences. As more women opt to pursue
careers, changes in traditional family patterns emerge. For example, the dual-career family has become more widespread, and the
ramifications of this kind of family structure are considered.

Key terms in this section:

critical event
fear of success

dual-career family

LEARNING OBJECTIVES

1.   What important life events characterize the period of young
    adulthood in our society? (p. 406)

2.   Describe the major features of physical development between
    the ages of 20 and 40. (pp. 406-408)

3. Describe how each of the following is related to better health in adulthood: (pp. 408-410)

   Lifestyle:

   Education:

   Gender:

   Marital status:

   Life stress:

4. Summarize how changes in women's hormonal levels can affect their emotions. (pp. 410-412)

5. Discuss the difference between fluid and crystallized intelligence. How does each of these change with age? (pp. 412-413)

6. Describe how young adults compare with older adults on tests
    of egocentrism? Explain what might account for any differ-
    ences. (p. 414)

7. Explain how one's experiences play an important role in moral
    development in adulthood. (pp. 414-415)

8. Trace the sequence of moral development of women according
    to Gilligan. (pp. 415-417)

    Level one:

        Transition:

    Level two:

        Transition:

Level three:

9. Describe how people of different professions differ in terms of when they are most productive and creative and list possible explanations for these differences. (p. 417)

10. List factors which seem to be important in job choice and satisfaction. (pp. 417-419)

11. Summarize the forces that have been important in producing disparities in the occupational status and income of men and women? (pp. 419-421)

12. Explain the term "fear of success" and describe the types of women most likely to display such a fear. (p. 420)

13. List the advantages and some of the strains that are experienced in a dual-career family and describe societal changes that could ease some of these strains. (pp. 421-422)

Advantages:

Strains:

Changes:

Circle the letter of the choice that completes each item.

1. The period of life between ages 20 and 40 is characterized by: (a) preparation for one's career goals; (b) a decline in one's physical abilities; (c) financial and emotional independence; (d) realignment of values and identity.

2. Generally speaking, the health of young adults is: (a) better than all other age groups in the population; (b) more seriously jeopardized by disease than any other cause; (c) about the same as it was during childhood; (d) significantly poorer than that of adolescents.

3. It has been found that fluctuations in a woman's hormonal levels seem to affect: (a) both emotional states and cognitive functioning; (b) emotional states but not cognitive functioning; (c) cognitive functioning but not emotional states; (d) weight and desire for physical activity.

4. Tests that measure vocabulary and general information are tapping: (a) fluid intelligence; (b) crystallized intelligence; (c) egocentrism; (d) transitivity.

5. Contrary to Piagetian theory, young adults have been found to show: (a) more egocentrism than older adults; (b) a great deal of

animistic reasoning; (c) poor performance on tests of transitivity; (d) a decline in conservation skills.

6.   Cecile has just developed a new moral attitude as a result of becoming pregnant. Before, she used to drink fairly heavily because she enjoyed it. Now she is concerned about the effect of alcohol on her unborn infant. So she decides to not drink until after the baby is born. Cecile exhibits what Gilligan calls: (a) level-one moral reasoning (individual survival); (b) level-two moral reasoning (self-sacrifice); (c) transition to level three; (d) transition to level two.

7.   In which of the following professions would creative work tend to come in later life? (a) musician; (b) writer; (c) poet; (d) scientist.

8.   People who are satisfied with their jobs tend to be those with: (a) high-status positions; (b) low-status positions; (c) less education; (d) high-paying jobs.

9.   In recent years, women who are in the job market in the United States: (a) have earned just as much money as men have; (b) have held the same types of jobs as men; (c) have worked for the same basic reasons that men have; (d) have been victims of conflict over their dual roles.

10.   Nonconformity, flexibility, and self-reliance are all characteristics of: (a) professional women; (b) women who hold low-status jobs; (c) married women; (d) women who are classified as "homemakers."

PRACTICE EXERCISES

Completion

Supply the words or phrases that best complete these sentences.

1.   With regard to physical development, _____muscular_____

_____ is at its peak between ages 25 and 30, followed by only a gradual decline in later years. Also, the

___senses___ are functioning most optimally in young
adulthood.

2.   The frequency of death from all causes rises dramatically

after the age of __30__ , with the death rate for

___males___ exceeding that for ___females___ . The

175

leading cause of death among young men is _____*accidents*_____ .

3. In general, it has been found that women display higher rates

    of accidents, suicides, and crime during the _____*pre menstrual*_____

    and _____ phases of their cycles. It is
    thought that changes in emotional states are products of vary-

    ing levels of _____ in the woman's body.

4. _____*Fluid*_____ intelligence involves conceptual reasoning
    and abstraction. This type of intelligence tends to

    _____*decline*_____ during adulthood.

5. Tests of vocabulary and general information are measures of

    _____*crystalline*_____ intelligence, which tends to

    _____↑_____ as an individual grows older.

6. Although we would not expect it, older adults tend to be

    _____*more*_____ egocentric than young adults on spatial per-

    ception tasks. This could be due to the fewer _____

    _____*social interaction*_____they experience or to some loss in

    _____*neurological*_____ functioning.

7. Advances in moral development are usually made when adults

    have experiences with strong _____*emotional*_____ components that
    cause a rethinking to occur.

8. Stockmal (1976) has found that very often a " _____*critical event*_____

    _____ " affects people's first jobs or their lifetime
    careers.

9. The fact that many capable women are afraid of demonstrating
    their competence in their vocations has been called

    " _____*fear of success*_____ ."

10. _____*Dual*_____ - _____*career*_____ families are those in which
    both the husband and wife pursue their vocational goals. The
    number of couples choosing this lifestyle appears to be

    _____↑_____ .

176

Matching

In the blank to the left of each definition, write the letter that indicates the term defined.

___e___ 1. Shows slight decline during young adulthood
___f___ 2. Leading cause of death under age 30
___d___ 3. Involves conceptual and·abstract thinking
___a___ 4. Intelligence based upon education and cultural background
___h___ 5. Cognitive feature in college students which is greater than it "should" be
___g___ 6. First level of moral reasoning for women
___i___ 7. Second level of moral reasoning for women
___j___ 8. What Stockmal sees as influencing career choice
___b___ 9. Alternative lifestyle that's on the increase
___c___ 10. Culturally based obstacle for professional women

a. crystallized
b. dual career
c. fear of success
d. fluid intelligence
e. manual dexterity

f. accidents
g. individual survival
h. animism
i. self-sacrifice
j. critical event

True-False

Circle T if the statement is true, F if the statement is false.

T **F** 1. Black and white men have about an equal chance of dying from homicide.

T F 2. Eating breakfast is related to good health.

T **F** 3. Despite possible specific problems, smoking is not related to general health in young adulthood.

T F 4. Fluid intelligence tends to decline through adulthood.

T F 5. Tests on Piagetian tasks show that old adults are more cognitively advanced than the typical 30-year-old.

T F 6. Cultural expectations may affect moral development in women.

T **F** 7. Gilligan proposes that self-sacrifice represents the highest level of moral development for women.

T **F** 8. Job satisfaction is primarily the result of pay level.

T **F** 9. Recent social and legal movements have eliminated the disproportionate distribution of men and women in specific occupations.

T (F) 10. There are really no advantages to a dual-career lifestyle.

SELF TEST B

Circle the letter of the choice that completes each item.

1. Young adults are usually: (a) at their peak physically and
intellectually; (b) less secure with their identity than they were
during adolescence; (c) no longer undergoing changes in personal
goals; (d) more prone to cardiovascular disease than are adolescents.

2. Physical development during the adult years includes: (a) a
gradual loss in muscular strength, beginning at age 20; (b) a substantial loss in visual acuity; (c) the stable functioning of most
of the senses; (d) increases in finger dexterity until age 50.

3. In general, people who are healthy tend to be: (a) less educated; (b) married; (c) males; (d) smokers.

4. Paige (1973) found that women from different cultural backgrounds: (a) all showed the same changes in moods during their
menstrual cycles; (b) varied in their mood changes, depending on
which culture they came from; (c) showed wide individual differences in mood changes that were unrelated to cultural background;
(d) all showed little or no mood change over time.

5. Past studies that have shown that intellectual abilities decline after the age of 20 may have been affected by: (a) cohort
differences; (b) the fact that they were longitudinal; (c) the
absence of reliable tests; (d) biases of young test writers.

6. In contrast to childhood and adolescence, moral development in
adulthood involves: (a) cognitive growth; (b) personal moral experiences; (c) training in moral principles; (d) peer interaction.

7. According to Gilligan, the highest level of moral reasoning
for women stresses: (a) self-sacrifice; (b) child rearing; (c)
self-preservation; (d) nonviolence.

8. Most people choose their lifetime careers: (a) in young adulthood or later; (b) in adolescence; (c) when they get their first
jobs; (d) during the youth period.

9. "Fear of success" has a higher incidence among women whose:
(a) fathers are successful professionals; (b) mothers are successful professionals; (c) fathers have not been successful; (d)
mothers worked outside the home.

10. Stresses for dual-career families can stem from the: (a) more egalitarian relationship between the husband and wife; (b) fact that several roles have to be filled by the husband and wife; (c) decreased capacity for each individual to develop; (d) increased financial burden incurred for babysitters, extra cars, and so on.

VIGNETTES

1. In college, many women are said to experience "fear of success." If you could change the college experience, what might you do to reduce this syndrome?

2. A 24-year-old friend of yours has decided not to take piano lessons because "adults cannot learn music as easily as children and besides their fingers are not as nimble as a youngster's." What might you say to change your friend's mind?

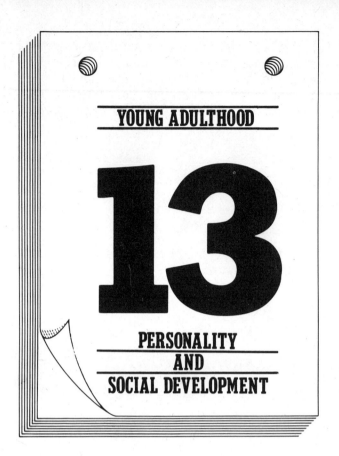

YOUNG ADULTHOOD

13

PERSONALITY
AND
SOCIAL DEVELOPMENT

INTEGRATOR

The search for one's identity, a central aspect of adolescence
(Chapter 11) is for the most part complete by young adulthood, and
the emphasis shifts to developing intimate interpersonal relationships. Reevaluation of one's life continues throughout the adult
years, and particularly during the middle-age years, when the
"midlife crisis" is said to occur (Chapter 15). This constant
change is seen by most theorists, such as Erikson and Buhler, as
being quite positive for healthy adjustment. Buhler's theory, introduced in this chapter, will be encountered again in Chapters 15
and 17 as will the last two stages of Erikson's theory.

During the young-adulthood years, choices are made regarding a
personal lifestyle which reflects personal development which has
preceded and which will influence development of the individual in
the years to come. Consideration of alternative lifestyles is included in this chapter.

OVERVIEW

Theoretical Perspectives on Adult Development

Two major theories of personality are presented. The first is
Buhler's theory, which views human development as occurring in five

180

stages, all centered on goal-setting behaviors. There is a progression from a general unawareness of one's life goals in childhood to an idealistic search for cosmic goals in adolescence and
young adulthood. By middle adulthood, people have set clearer and
more specific goals for themselves and enjoy a rich personal life.
Buhler's theory proposes that self-fulfillment is the key to successful growth.

Erikson's next stage of development is the second theory considered.
Erikson sees the young adult as being in the process of resolving
the conflict between intimacy and isolation. In this stage, the
person must fuse his or her identity with another person in a
close, trusting relationship; otherwise, isolation and self-
absorption can result. Resolution of this crisis makes true genitality possible. The theory is limited in that it advocates only
heterosexual sex that culminates in mutual orgasm and ultimately
leads to procreation.

Key terms in this section:

self-fulfillment   heterosexual sex
intimacy vs. isolation   mutual orgasm
true genitality   procreation

Research Studies of Adult Development

Although there is wide variation in personality among adults, research findings offer some general insights into the personality
function of adults. The text presents three major studies that
have been concerned with this issue. The Grant study of men showed
that the focus of concern for adult males tends to shift as they
leave home and establish an independent family life. Transitions
in focus from wife, to job, to children are common throughout the
period. The Levinson studies of men also detailed transitions
throughout adulthood and outlined five stages of adult development
for men. During the final stage a man discards the mentor role
and develops according to one of three sequences. The Gould
studies included women as well as men. For both groups, four age-
related periods are described in which adults become increasingly
settled in their lifestyle.

Choosing a Personal Lifestyle

The next major section enumerates the several lifestyles that are
chosen by different young adults and the consequences each can have
for the individual. Romantic love is a complex phenomenon. Factors associated with choosing a mate are diverse and complex.
Proximity, similarity, and balance seem to be related to choosing
a mate. Researchers have identified six components of love: affective, cognitive, physical, verbal, behavioral and fantasy. Love
relationships are classified as passionate and companionate.

Marriage is the most popular lifestyle for adults in the United States. Predicting success in marriage is difficult, but several important factors include: age of partners, religious match, personality factors, and husbands' characteristics. Emotional growth and other benefits of marriage are discussed. Marriages can be generally classified as conflict-habituated, devitalized, passive-congenial, vital, or total.

Sexuality is an important aspect of adult life. Marital sex is generally more satisfying and frequent today than in times past. Sexual development in marriage is an important component in the relationship. Extramarital sex has remained fairly constant with the greatest change being with men and women under 25 years of age.

Violence between spouses has only recently been brought into public view, and data are scarce. Violence seems to be related to unemployment and cultural values.

Some people choose to remain single, and the positive and negative sides of this pattern of living are presented. Schwaltz found that singles are a diverse group in which six patterns or types of lifestyle could be identified. These were the professional, social, individualistic, activist, passive, and supportive patterns. One new social arrangement that has emerged among single people is cohabitation. Like marriage, this social structure can have both positive and negative consequences for the individual.

A major development stage that many adults experience is parenthood. The birth of a baby marks a major transition point for the parents. The first child brings new responsibilities and social roles. The reactions of the father and mother are different but equally far reaching. The choice to have children is discussed next. Today's adults have opted for smaller families but continue to have children, reflecting what Erikson calls generativity. Factors associated with choosing parenthood are considered as are the effects of children on the parents' marriage. Four phases of parenthood are outlined, each of which involves a new role for the parents. These phases are: anticipation, honeymoon, plateau, and disengagement.

Changes in styles of parenting are considered, with emphasis on significant changes in the roles of fathers and in stepparenting. The implications of the new father role and of the reconstituted (or blended) family members are discussed. Many more adults today opt for nonparenthood. This choice also entails advantages as well as stresses; both are considered.

The last portion of this section discusses divorce--a phenomenon on the rise in our society. Besides discussing some of the reasons for this increase, this section details some of the consequences that divorce has on the emotional status of people. According to

Bohannan, the process of divorce has six aspects: emotional, legal, economic, coparental, community, and psychic. A successful divorce involves a mutual awareness and positive separation.

Key terms in this section:

mentor	vital marriage
romantic love	total marriage
passionate love	cohabitation
companionate love	generativity
conflict-habituated marriage	stepparenting
devitalized marriage	reconstituted (blended) family
passive-congenial marriage	successful divorce

Friendship in Young Adulthood

Friendships continue to be important in adulthood. Establishing a new friendship may recapitulate the development sequence described by Selman and Selman, though most adults have difficulty in moving from Stage 3 (intimacy) to Stage 4 (autonomy). Factors affecting choice of friends are discussed.

LEARNING OBJECTIVES

1. Describe the central feature of human development, according to Buhler. (p. 426)

2. Outline the events which mark the two adult stages of development, as outlined by Buhler. (p. 426)

3. Describe how Erikson characterizes the young adult who has successfully resolved the intimacy-versus-isolation crisis and indicate whether the research on adult development agrees or disagrees with his theoretical ideas. (p. 427)

4. Briefly describe the findings of the Grant study of adult development. (pp. 427-428)

5. List and briefly describe the five stages of life that adult males go through according to Levinson and his colleagues. (pp. 429-431)

   a.

   b.

   c.

   d.

   e.

6. Describe three sequences of development during Levinson's fifth (boom) stage. (p. 431)

7. Describe the sequences of development identified by Gould. (pp. 431-432)

8. Review factors associated with falling in love. (pp. 432-433)

9. List and define the six components of love investigated by Neiswender, Birren, and Schase. (p. 433)

   a.

   b.

   c.

d.

e.

f.

10. Cite three criteria that researchers have used to appraise
    the success of a marriage and discuss the problems associated
    with using each of these criteria. (p. 434)

    a.

    b.

    c.

11. List five predictors of a successful marriage. (pp. 434-435)

    a.

    b.

    c.

d.

e.

12. Explain how marriage can contribute to a person's emotional development. (p. 435)

13. List four benefits that marriage offers to individuals in our society. (pp. 435-436)

a.

b.

c.

d.

14. List and describe five types of marriages identified by Cuber and Harroff (1965). (pp. 436-437)

a.

b.

c.

d.

e.

15. Describe the influences that have been involved in making
    sexual activity a more vital part of married life. (pp. 437-
    439)

16. Discuss some advantages and disadvantages of being single in
    our society. (p. 440)

17. List and briefly describe six patterns of single living iden-
    tified by Schwartz. (pp. 441-442)

    a.

b.

c.

d.

e.

f.

18. Describe some of the benefits and problems that cohabitation can bring to the individuals involved. (pp. 443-444)

19. Describe the impact of a first baby on the mother, on the father, and on the marriage. (pp. 444-446)

Mother:

Father:

Marriage:

20. Discuss some reasons why some people might decide to have children and why others decide not to. (pp. 446-447; 453-454)

21. List and describe four phases of parenthood. (p. 449)

    a.

    b.

    c.

    d.

22. Discuss how the role of fathering has changed in recent years. (pp. 449-451)

23. Discuss the stresses involved in stepparenting. (pp. 451-453)

24. Cite factors that seem to contribute to the rising divorce rate in our society. (pp. 454-455)

25. Describe the six components of divorce enumerated by Bohannan. (pp. 455-456)

   a.

   b.

   c.

   d.

   e.

   f.

26. Describe the process of obtaining a successful divorce. (p. 455)

27. List factors which contribute to friendships in adulthood and the possible functions of friends. (pp. 456-457)

SELF TEST A

Circle the letter of the choice that completes each item.

1. According to Buhler, the key to healthy development is: (a) self-fulfillment; (b) the resolution of the intimacy-versus-isolation conflict; (c) achieving independence; (d) intimacy.

2. In general, research on young adulthood has: (a) verified Erikson's contention that the individual has found his identity by this time; (b) refuted Erikson's contention that the individual has found his identity by this time; (c) supported Erikson's feeling that career development occurs largely in adolescence; (d) refuted Erikson's contention that adults search for intimacy.

3. Tom, a 27-year-old, is torn between proposing marriage to a girl he loves and his desire to be able to travel at any time to advance his career as a photographer. Tom would most likely be classified by Levinson as being in: (a) a becoming-one's-own-man stage; (b) a settling down stage; (c) Stage 1, leaving the family; (d) Stage 2, getting into the adult world.

4. It has been found that the success of a marriage is most influenced by the: (a) background and adjustment of the husband; (b) background and adjustment of the wife; (c) financial status of the couple; (d) the number and spacing of children.

5. Cid and Mable fight almost continually, but they do not see their fighting as a problem. Theirs is a(n): (a) conflict-

habituated marriage; (b) devitalized marriage; (c) abuse-oriented marriage; (d) total marriage.

6. The largest increase in extramarital sexual activity has been among: (a) women between 18 and 24; (b) men between 30 and 40; (c) women between 30 and 40; (d) men between 40 and 50.

7. Complaints of physical abuse in a marriage are: (a) more common among lower-class women; (b) more common among middle class women; (c) very rare; (d) found to the same degree in all cultures.

8. Which of the following statements is true regarding parenthood? (a) There is no basis for viewing parenthood as a separate developmental stage. (b) Although couples are still having children, they are having fewer. (c) Parenting results in the growth of children while parents themselves change very little. (d) Deciding not to have children provides no clear advantages.

9. A "successful" divorce: (a) always involves a period of adjustment; (b) rarely involves a period of adjustment; (c) depends only on how the divorce was handled; (d) is one that eventually leads to reconciliation.

10. Dan and Alice have two children, ages 6 and 11. They would be considered to be in which stage of parenthood? (a) honeymoon; (b) anticipation; (c) disengagement; (d) plateau.

PRACTICE EXERCISES

Completion

Supply the words or phrases that best complete these sentences.

1. The Grant study found that for men in their 30's, their

   _____careers_____ were the focal points of their lives. The best predictor of success in this area was whether or not the

   person had a stable __personality__ .

2. __Buhler__ outlined five stages of development through the life span, emphasizing that goal setting and

   __self fulfillment__ were the major vehicles of healthy growth.

3. According to Erikson, it is only when the crisis between

   __intimacy__ and __isolation__ is resolved that "true genitality" can occur. Ideally, the individual strives for _____mutual_____ _____reason_____ with another,

which ultimately leads to _____procreation._____ .

4. A marriage is more likely to be successful if people marry in
their late _____20's_____ or later. Also, the success rate
is higher if both partners are of the same _____religion_____ and
_____social_____ _____class_____ .

5. A marriage that is characterized by constant quarreling and
nagging might be termed _____conflict - habit_____ . A
_____total_____ marriage is one where togetherness dominates
the entire lives of the couple.

6. Infidelity has been found to occur in every type of marriage
except the _____total_____ marriage.

7. Unmarried couples who live together openly are said to be
_____cohabitating_____ . The number of couples choosing such a
lifestyle appears to be _____↑_____ .

8. A significant transition point in a married couple's lives
is _____parenthood_____ , when the major familial reference
point changes and new responsibilities arise.

9. The phase of parenthood in which the active parental role ends
has been called _____disengagement_____ .

10. Although a divorce may be successful, there is always a period
of _____adjustment_____ that follows.

True-False

Circle T if the statement is true, F if the statement is false.

T (F) (1.) According to Buhler, adults form specific goals between
ages 23 and 45.

T (F) 2. Major research studies show that the focus of concern
is stable and shifts very little during adulthood.

(T) F 3. The experience of love rests primarily on affective,
           cognitive, physical, and verbal components.

T (F) 4. Today it is fairly easy to predict success or failure
           in marriage.

(T) F 5. Crisis resolution can serve as a clear benefit of mar-
           riage.

(T) F 6. A vital marriage is one in which the partners have
           separate identities but enjoy each other and their
           relationship.

(T) F (7) Extramarital sex has risen steadily in the last fifteen
            years.

(T) F 8. The role of fathers is currently undergoing change and
           is starting to include share-childrearing.

(T) F 9. An individualistic single person focuses on his or her
           own self-identity.

T (F) 10. Once an adult finds a suitable mate, friendships decline
            in number and lose their importance.

SELF TEST B

Circle the letter of the choice that completes each item.

1. In Buhler's theory of development, people are idealistic and
search for life's goals during: (a) childhood; (b) adolescence and
young adulthood; (c) middle adulthood; (d) old age.

2. Erikson's theory of development during adulthood: (a) is
restricted to heterosexual relationships; (b) is restricted to
sexual accomplishment; (c) states that trust can be shared prior
to finding one's identity; (d) is totally supported by research
data.

3. Mary seems to have achieved her career goal by becoming district
manager of a large retail outlet chain. Yet Mary sees herself as
a failure. This is a pattern which Levinson called: (a) ritual-
ized failure; (b) breaking out; (c) advancement with stability;
(d) failure-decline.

4. Kip says he loves Susan because she is easy to talk to and he
can confide in her. Kip is exhibiting which component of romantic
love? (a) cognitive; (b) affective; (c) fantasy; (d) verbal.

5. People who marry each other tend to be: (a) in their 30's or
older when they wed; (b) from the same educational background;
(c) of different socioeconomic classes; (d) very dissimilar physically.

6. Which of the following is not related to success in marriage?
(a) age of man and woman; (b) similarity of religion; (c) husband's
adjustment; (d) number of premarital sexual experiences.

7. The state of marriage: (a) can take many different forms,
depending on the couple's patterns of behavior; (b) in almost all
cases involves the same patterns of behavior between couples; (c)
can change from one type or pattern to another quite often; (d) is
more fulfilling for a woman.

8. The lifestyle of remaining single, at least in young adulthood:
(a) has become increasingly popular; (b) has become increasingly
unpopular; (c) offers more disadvantages than advantages for the
individual; (d) ensures little or no sexual activity.

9. A recent development in the nature of parenthood is that:
(a) the extended-family structure is being widely used to ease the
strains of parenting; (b) mothers are assuming a more dominant role
in caring for their children; (c) fathers are playing a more active
role in parenting; (d) families are getting larger and sibling
caretakers are often used.

10. The present increase in the divorce rate is: (a) a sign that
people don't want to be married; (b) largely the result of people's
higher expectations for marriage; (c) lowest among the group of
young adults; (d) the result of poor child rearing by past parental
generations.

VIGNETTES

1. Most college students are "novice adults." From the information presented in this chapter, how would you describe the "typical"
college student?

2. Violence between spouses is a troublesome social phenomenon.
If you were asked to cite what you consider to be the major causes
of family violence, what might you mention.

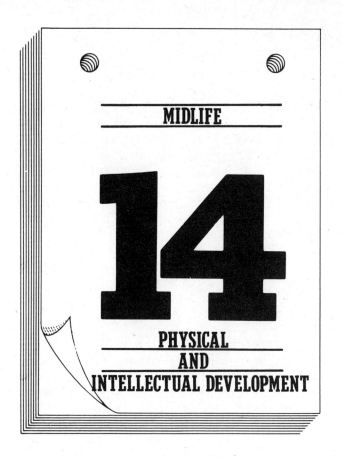

MIDLIFE

14

PHYSICAL
AND
INTELLECTUAL DEVELOPMENT

INTEGRATOR

In Chapter 12, we learned that young adulthood is characterized by physical robustness and general good health. In this chapter, we will see that during the middle years of adulthood good health and vitality as a general rule continue. Certain specific physical changes will occur, and this chapter discusses these changes and ways in which adults deal with them. Continuing good health will be shown to be an important factor in the personality and social development during midlife as well as during old age, which will be considered in Chapters 15 and 17. The intellectual functioning of the midlife adult will also be considered. Decline in intellectual functioning is very rare in this age group, and improved IQ and conservation skills are often noted. The impact of continuing education and career shifts will also be considered. The capacity to continue in a productive mode is more likely for those who continue to be educated and, as we shall see, can be an important variable of adjustment in old age.

OVERVIEW

Physical Functioning in Middle Age

Middle age is difficult to define precisely. The chapter discusses some of the general events which are normally associated
with this period and considers the difficulty of applying a set
age span as middle age. For purposes of discussion, the text
chooses ages 40 to 65 as a useful age description of midlife.
While the trend in physical capacity is downward during the middle
years, very few individuals experience declines significant enough
to warrant drastic changes in activities. The general physical condition during these years is good with a decline in reserve capacity
as the major change. Physical capacity is related to lifestyle,
with those individuals following the seven basic health practices
outlined in Table 12-1 in the text enjoying better health. Certain
diseases related to lifestyle and obesity are major health problems
for some during this period.

Men and women show different patterns of health with certain ailments more likely for one sex or the other. Men have a higher death
rate than women during this period. Cultural factors are considered
which may contribute to these differences. One significant biological event in women's lives during this period is menopause.
Brought on by a series of physiological events known collectively
as climacteric and which reduce estrogen production, this event
signals the cessation of reproductive capability for the woman. An
array of symptoms of menopause are discussed with consideration of
their hormonal basis. Men also experience hormonal fluctuations
during this period, and this may affect the nature of sexual activity. While males retain reproductive capacity well into old age,
a male climacteric has been proposed to describe some of the biological changes which occur.

Sensory functioning declines slowly but steadily throughout the
midlife period. Declines in vision, hearing, taste, and smell are
described. Psychomotor skills do not necessarily decline, while
10 percent loss in total strength is typical. Complex motor skills,
in particular, may remain stable or improve during the middle years.

Adults must deal with the physical changes, whether large or small,
that occur and they do so in many different ways. The exact degree
and style of coping seems to be largely idiosyncratic except that
the double standard of aging may cause women to be more upset about
growing older than men.

Key terms in this section:

reserve capacity   male climacteric
menopause   double standard of aging
climacteric

Intellectual Functioning in Middle Age

The next section gives an account of intellectual functioning
during midlife. Contrary to some beliefs, IQ scores tend to increase at least until the mid-fifties. The problems of using tests
designed for children and differences in motivation for children
and adults is considered and calls into question the utility of
testing adult IQ's. Performance of adults on tests tends to show
increases in several areas, especially those relating to verbal
abilities. Interesting gender differences also emerge and are
discussed.

In tests of Piagetian cognitive functioning, middle-aged adults
show considerable variability on some tasks and little on others.
Strong areas tend to include conservation and classification.
Solving formal operational problems is more variable and seems to
reflect past life experiences of the individual. Continued moral
development is possible throughout adulthood, and creativity tends
to be a hallmark characteristic of the midlife period.

Continuing education is a phenomenon which is on the rise in
America. Adults are going back to school in increasing numbers
each year. A description of the adult learner includes a good
basic education, high income, and an age range of 34 to 44. The
reasons for continuing education are numerous. The decision is
often career related but not always.

The chapter concludes with a discussion of career adjustment during
midlife. Career orientation during this period tends to be one of
two kinds. Either the person is at the peak of the career he or
she chose in young adulthood, or he or she shifts to a new vocation
and is just starting a new career. Levinson has proposed the construct life structure to account for shifts in a person's goals of
participation in society. Thomas has further proposed that combinations of changes or persistence in career and/or life structure
can be used to classify people as changers, pseudo-changers, crypto-
changers, or persisters. The text considers events which may encourage a person to change including the completion of child rearing,
financial concerns, or anxiety. As more adults shift careers, the
importance of training programs will grow.

Key terms in this section:

adult learner   pseudo-changer
life structure   crypto-changer
changer   persister

199

LEARNING OBJECTIVES

1. Discuss some of the definitions that have been offered for the term "middle age." (p. 462)

2. Describe the general nature of the health of middle-aged adults. (pp. 463-465)

3. Discuss the different attitudes of men and women toward their health. (pp. 465-466)

4. List several changes directly linked to the reduction of estrogen production during menopause and those changes which seem to be more psychologically based. (p. 466)

5. Describe the changes associated with male climacteric. (p. 467)

6. Briefly describe what happens to sensory functioning during the middle-adult years in terms of vision, hearing, smell, and taste. (pp. 467-468)

7. Discuss differences of complex motor skills as compared to simple motor skill performance during middle age. (p. 468)

8. Describe the content and impact of the "double standard of aging." (pp. 468-469)

9. Describe the effects of lifestyle and sex on health during middle adulthood. (pp. 465-466)

10. Describe the general performance of middle-aged adults on IQ tests. (pp. 469-470)

11. Describe some problems associated with assessing adult IQ. (p. 469)

12. Describe the functioning of middle-aged adults on Piagetian tasks of cognitive functioning. (p. 470)

13. List and briefly discuss the factors which seem to be related to the recent increase in adult education. (p. 472)

14. Describe two general patterns of career adjustment in midlife. (p. 472)

    a.

    b.

15. Describe what is meant by the term "life structure." (p. 473)

16. List and describe four categories proposed by Thomas to classify people who vary in career and life-structure changes.
(p. 473)

a.

b.

c.

d.

17. Describe some common events which occur during midlife which
may influence a person's career or life structure. (p. 474)

SELF TEST A

Circle the letter of the choice that completes each item.

1. A major change during middle adulthood involves: (a) increases
in heart rate; (b) decreases in reserve capacity; (c) increases in
kidney capacity; (d) decreases in chest size.

2. Which of the following is <u>not</u> usually a major contributing

factor to health problems during the middle adult years? (a) obesity; (b) smoking; (c) overuse of alcohol; (d) overuse of drugs.

3. Insomnia, fatigue, and anxiety during menopause: (a) are known to be caused by decreased hormone production; (b) may result from middle age itself; (c) are rare symptoms; (d) are signals for other health problems.

4. Which of the following is not a part of the male climacteric? (a) sterility; (b) decreased testosterone production; (c) decreased frequency of orgasm; (d) increases in impotency.

5. Of the following, the most common occurrence during middle age is: (a) nearsightedness; (b) deafness; (c) loss of some taste ability; (d) improvement in simple motor tasks.

6. Harold is a middle-aged male. We would expect him to exhibit his greatest decrease in ability when: (a) driving a car; (b) working on a lathe at home in his shop; (c) sorting mail at work; (d) responding quickly to a light at an intersection.

7. IQ scores in middle age: (a) decline sharply by the age of 50; (b) increase until the mid-fifties; (c) show no change from previous years; (d) decline only in verbal scores.

8. Katie is a 45-year-old woman. In which of the following tasks would we expect her to outperform her 20-year-old daughter? (a) conservation tasks; (b) classification tasks; (c) formal operational thinking; (d) egocentric communication.

9. Middle-aged adults who return to school tend to: (a) come from lower socioeconomic groups; (b) be at least 55 years of age; (c) have had a good education already; (d) earn about $10,000 annually.

10. Denise is a 50-year-old woman who until now has remained single and worked as an account executive for a legal firm. She has just gotten married and has quit her job in order to pursue a lifelong desire to be a professional painter. She and her new husband are also very involved in the raising of his three children from a previous marriage. Denise could best be classified as a: (a) persister; (b) changer; (c) crypto-changer; (d) pseudo-changer.

PRACTICE EXERCISES

Completion

Supply the words or phrases that best complete these sentences.

1. Middle age is considered to be the stage between ages

_____ and _____. A central aspect of this time is

the _____ of one's self and one's life goals.

2. Although middle-aged adults usually suffer from a variety of

   ailments, these are usually _____. _____
   are typically more anxious about their own health, while

   _____ are more anxious about protecting their
   spouse's health than their own.

3. The ability to perform _____ motor skills generally
   declines during middle age. However, some skills, such as

   driving, improve because _____ makes up for
   decrements in ability.

4. The _____ is the period during which physiological changes that bring about menopause take place.

5. Many symptoms of menopause, such as "hot flashes," are linked

   to the decreased production of _____. Similarly,

   men experience a decreased production of _____,
   which brings on biological changes.

6. Sexual activity continues, although it is _____ in
   the middle years, partly because of biological changes in males.

7. The fact that men are allowed to age without penalty while

   women are not is an indication of the _____

   _____ of aging in our society.

8. Longitudinal studies have shown that IQ scores _____

   at least until the _____.

9. Adults in middle age generally show high levels of

   _____ ability on Piagetian tasks. However, not

   all middle-aged adults can solve _____

   _____ problems.

10. An increasing tendency for adults to pursue _____

    _____ is probably due to the desire to prepare
    for career changes or to expand skills and knowledge.

True-False

Circle T if the statement is true, F if the statement is false.

T F   1.   Middle age is often a time of reevaluation of life goals.

T F   2.   There are really no significant physical changes associated with midlife.

T F   3.   Lifestyle has been associated with the incidence of anemia, heart disease, and cancer of the cervix in middle adulthood.

T F   4.   There is clearly no such thing as a male climacteric.

T F   5.   All the so-called symptoms of menopause are psychological rather than physical.

T F   6.   During the middle-adult years, there is a gradual decline in vision, hearing, and taste.

T F   7.   Adults all tend to cope with physical changes in much the same way.

T F   8.   Data clearly indicate that while intelligence declines during the midlife period, creativity is at a peak.

T F   9.   Most adults who go back to school tend to be well educated and of respectable income groups.

T F 10.   Crypto-changers are people who change jobs but otherwise keep their lives pretty much the same.

Word Scrambler

Unscramble the ten items. Then arrange the circled letters to finish the sentence below.

1. _ _ _ _ _ _ _ _ _ _ _ _ ◯

    E F L I T T U R C E U S R

    Goals of life participation

2. _ _ _ ◯ _ _ _ _ _ _ _

    I T E C C M C L I A R

    Leads to menopause

3. _ _ _ _ _ ◯ _ _

    S E O R G E T N

    Decreases during menopause

4. _ _ _ _ _ _ _ _ _ _Ⓞ_

Y O R T N C E P C R A G H

Change in life goals but not career

5. _ _ _Ⓞ_ _ _ _ _ _

R E I C T I V A T Y

At high point during midlife

6. _ _ _ _Ⓞ_ _ _ _

I E S R T P R S E

Keeps life as it is

7. _ _ _ _Ⓞ_ _ _ _ _ _ _ _

S A D H P N E O G U C E R

Changes career only

8. _ _ _ _ _ _ _

O X C E P M L

Motor skill undiminished during midlife

9. Ⓞ_ _ _ _ _ _ _ _ _ _ _ _

B U D O L E T A R S D N A D

Social bias regarding aging

10. _ _ _ _ _Ⓞ

L O A F M R

Type of operational thought that is variable among middle-agers

Though it is difficult to define exactly, the period between

40 and 65 years is often called _ _ _ _ _ _

_ _ _.

SELF TEST B

Circle the letter of the choice that completes each item.

1. Middle age has been defined as a: (a) time when people focus on the future; (b) time period between ages 25 and 35; (c) period of reevaluation of self; (d) period of decline in marriage satisfaction.

2. A loss in reserve capacity does not include: (a) gastrointestinal secretion; (b) decreased pumping capacity of the heart; (c) increased chest size; (d) loss of size in the prostrate gland.

3. Which of the following health problems is more typical of women: (a) heart disease; (b) anemia; (c) ulcers; (d) emphysema.

4. Menopause is caused by a decrease in: (a) estrogen; (b) sexual activity; (c) testosterone; (d) adrenalin.

5. Hearing loss during middle adulthood: (a) is very rare; (b) is almost always noticed as it limits the person's ability to function; (c) varies for different cultures; (d) amounts to about 35 percent by the age of 40.

6. The double standard of aging refers to a: (a) recent trend toward slower aging compared to the standards of earlier generations; (b) greater acceptability of aging by whites as compared to blacks; (c) greater acceptability of the opinions and values of youth compared to older Americans; (d) greater acceptability of aging in males than in females.

7. Tests of intelligence: (a) are not truly appropriate for adults; (b) are totally reliable for adults; (c) are totally useless for adults; (d) take into consideration the differing motivational levels of those tested.

8. Life structure includes concerns over: (a) physical well-being; (b) accumulation of material goods; (c) goals and roles in society; (d) declining physical appearance.

9. A person who changes careers but does not change other aspects of the life structure is classified as a: (a) changer; (b) persister; (c) pseudo-changer; (d) crypto-changer.

10. Elements that are not related to making a career shift include: (a) the emptying of the nest; (b) boredom with the old job; (c) financial concerns; (d) guilt over earning a large salary for less work.

VIGNETTES

1. Your father has just called to say "hello." In the course of the conversation, he mentions some concern over your mother's recent irritability, loss of sleep, and general anxiety. He concludes that it's all because "she's going through the change." Would you agree?

2. If you were working at an employment agency and were assigned a caseload of ten middle-aged individuals, what characteristics

would you expect them to exhibit? What would be your major concern
for your clients?

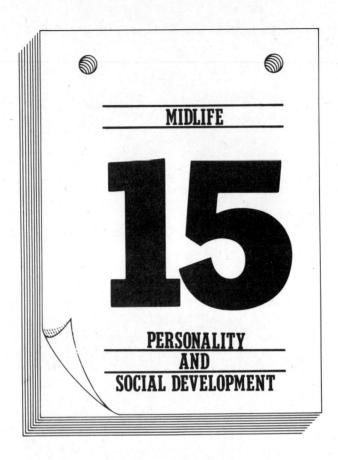

MIDLIFE

15

PERSONALITY
AND
SOCIAL DEVELOPMENT

In Chapter 15, we will consider the personality and social development that takes place during the middle-adulthood years. As in previous chapters, we will consider the development of self-concepts in adults and consider various theories of personality. The theories of Erikson and Buhler, which were introduced in preceding chapters, will again be examined as they apply to this developmental period. These will be supplemented by the introduction of Peck's theory and the social-psychological theory of Maslow. In Chapter 17, we will consider each of these orientations again as they focus on the period of old age.

The chapter will also consider research relating to midlife personality. The data of Grant, Gould, and Levinson which was first introduced in Chapter 13 will again have great relevancy. The topics of sex differences and family relationships will continue to be recurring themes in Chapter 15. Finally, the chapter will end with a description of friendship patterns as they have evolved from childhood (Chapters 5, 7, and 8), into adolescence (Chapter 11) and young adulthood (Chapter 13).

OVERVIEW

Self-Concept and Theoretical Perspectives of Middle Age

Personality continues to grow and change in the middle-adulthood
years. As these changes take place, alterations in self-concept
occur. On the whole, middle-agers see themselves in a positive
way. They are often busy with their reevaluation of themselves and
tend to see themselves as a bridge between generations. They enjoy
power and competence on the job and have a wealth of experience
upon which to draw in dealing with life situations.

A number of theoretical perspectives have been offered to describe
the personality functioning of the middle-aged adult. Erikson sees
the crises of generativity versus stagnation as the central issue
during this period. Peck has expanded upon Erikson's basic notion
and specifies four psychological developments as critical for successful adjustment in middle age. These are: valuing wisdom versus
valuing physical powers, socializing versus sexualizing in human
relations, cathectic flexibility versus cathectic impoverishment,
and mental flexibility versus mental rigidity. Buhler's fourth
phase involves taking stock of one's past to plan one's future
goals. This is thought to be the central focus during the middle
adulthood years. This reevaluation process leads to a feeling of
fulfillment or disappointment. The social-psychological view of
Maslow postulates that adult personality growth and development is
the product of changing life situations. This outlook stresses
flexibility as a keynote aspect of a healthy personality.

Key terms in this section:

generativity vs. stagnation	cathectic flexibility vs.
valuing wisdom vs. physical	impoverishment
powers	mental flexibility vs. rigidity
socializing vs. sexualizing	social-psychological view
in human relations	

Research in Personality Development in Midlife

Several attempts have been made to identify a few personality
characteristics that could be used to describe the typical middle-
ager. With the exception of introversion, which seems to increase
with age, the various studies have varied so much that it is impossible to draw any conclusions based upon their often contradictory conclusions. Methodological problems such as cohort effects
and lack of independence in personality dimensions call past findings into greater question. Coping styles have also been studied.
The way in which a person adapts to a crisis is affected by the life
stage they are in with off-time events causing more problems for
numerous reasons. The personality of the individual is also of
importance. In addition, since we are not yet an age-irrelevant
society, cultural expectations can make dealing with off-time events

more difficult. Clear sex differences in attitudes and coping
styles are also reported. The text delineates some of these differences and considers social factors which might contribute to
them.

A popular concept that has been proposed to describe middle-aged
personality is the midlife crisis. Lore predicts that this period
is one of tumultuous reexamination of one's goals, strengths and
weaknesses--often associated with drastic changes in personality
and behavior. The text reviews research by Levinson, Grant, and
Gould which supports the notion of a transition around age 40, but
does not predict that it will be a painful experience in most
cases. Other researchers such as Nydegger find no support for a
midlife crisis. Layton and Siegler propose that if there is a
midlife crisis it arises from the same three elements which are
found to operate at other life stages: identity, efficacy, and
self-evaluation. The loss of efficacy is said to promote crisis.
The displaced homemaker is offered as a case in point. Brim further proposes that crisis is more likely when the life situation
presents multiple stressors which extend beyond the individual's
coping capability.

Key terms in this section:

coping styles   identity
off-time events   efficacy
age-irrelevant society   self-evaluation
midlife crisis   displaced homemaker

Happiness in Early and Middle Adulthood

Happiness is a difficult construct to define. The best step is
to ask people if they are happy. The text reviews numerous factors
which seem to be related to reported happiness. Race and health
emerge as important variables as does gender, which affects both
the level and the timing of greatest happiness.

Family Relations

The next section considers a number of aspects of the family relationships in middle age and how these change and influence the individual. The focus is on marriage first. Today, couples who
remain together can anticipate some 20 years together after the last
child has left the home. Research into what these relationships
are like has yielded contradictory results. Pineo proposes that
they are marked by a gradual decline called disenchantment while
Burt disagrees and proposes periodic fluctuations in marital satisfaction. Adults in the launching stage, for example, report very
high marital satisfaction second only to honeymooners. Troll and
Smith attempt to reformulate the questions being asked by proposing
that the focus in marriage changes from attraction to attachment.

Thus the relationship changes in quality, not necessarily in quantity, of affection.

Sexuality is another important issue. Cultural expectations cause many adults to unnecessarily limit their sexual activities during the midlife period. Sexuality is different during this period due to changes in the male sexual response. This does not mean that sexuality is or should be absent. While most of the blocks to sexuality at this stage are nonphysiologic, steps can be taken to help couples who are aware of both cultural and physical obstacles to fulfilling sex lives.

Parenthood is still an important issue during this period. The middle-aged parents usually have adolescents who are themselves undergoing a period of some stress. Parents may experience a re-awakening of their own adolescent conflicts which can result in an overidentification with the child. Such a strong reaction does not mesh well with the adolescent's striving for autonomy. Other parenting issues include de-illusionment and the empty nest syndrome, which may or may not be a crisis period for the parents. In addition to being parents themselves, the middle-aged adults are also the children of aging parents. Midlife is a period in which abrupt changes occur in the parent-child relationship. The middle-aged child is able to be more objective in its view of its parents and a shift in dependency, with the aging parents becoming more dependent upon the middle-aged children, contributes to this change.

The heavy commitments to family, job, and life goals during the middle years of adulthood often leave little time for friendship. Friendships still persist during this period, but the emphasis is clearly placed on other aspects of the life situation. The establishment of new friendships is less dependent upon proximity and convenience during this stage but these factors still play a role.

Key terms in this section:

launching stage	de-illusionment
disenchantment	empty nest syndrome
attraction vs. attachment	

LEARNING OBJECTIVES

1. Describe the general self-concept of the middle-aged adult and list factors which are related to this self-image. (pp. 478-479)

2. Discuss the events that occur during midlife, according to Erikson. (pp. 479-480)

3. Contrast the adult who achieves generativity and the adult who stagnates. (pp. 479-480)

4. List four psychological developments that are seen by Peck as being important to successful emotional adjustment in middle age. (p. 480)

   a.

   b.

   c.

   d.

5. Discuss the events which occur during midlife, according to Buhler. (pp. 480-481)

6. List factors that affect adult personality growth according to the social-psychological point of view. (p. 481)

7. Define "coping style" and explain how each of the following can affect an adult's coping. (pp. 482-483)

Coping style is:

Off-time events:

Cultural expectations:

Individual personality:

Gender:

8. Describe what is meant by "midlife crisis" and discuss the factors which seem to be related to this phenomenon. (pp. 484-485)

9. Review the research data which supports the concept of mid-life crisis. (pp. 485-486)

10. Review the research data which does not support the existence of a midlife crisis. (pp. 485-487)

11. Describe Layton and Siegler's view of the midlife crisis. (pp. 487-488)

12. Describe the factors which seem to be related to happiness during the middle-adulthood period. (pp. 489-491)

13. Contrast the differing views of changes in the marital rela-
    tionship during the middle-adulthood years. (pp. 492-493)

14. Discuss the factors which contribute to decreased sexuality
    during the middle-aged period. (pp. 493-494)

15. Describe the special problems and tasks of parenthood asso-
    ciated with the midlife period. (pp. 494-496)

16. Describe the relative role of friendships during the middle
    adulthood period. (p. 497)

SELF TEST A

Circle the letter of the choice that completes each item.

1. Personality in midlife: (a) is not different from childhood;

(b) is not different from adolescence; (c) continues to change; (d) remains stable unless crises develop.

2. The self-concept of middle-aged adults is: (a) generally favorable; (b) generally unfavorable; (c) not fully formed; (d) often unrealistic.

3. According to Erikson, the main objective during middle adulthood is to: (a) acquire a sense of self-identity; (b) resolve conflicts over job and family life; (c) develop a desire to guide future generations; (d) become self-absorbed.

4. Joe is very depressed because he is now 50 years old and although he knows his job very well, he is painfully aware that he moves more slowly and with less vigor than in his younger years. According to Peck, Joe has failed to develop: (a) cathectic flexibility; (b) mental flexibility; (c) socializing in human relations; (d) a value of wisdom.

5. Personality is seen as a continual adjustment to changing social situations by a theory proposed by: (a) Erikson; (b) Maslow; (c) Buhler; (d) Peck.

6. Research has consistently shown that one personality dimension tends to increase during the midlife period. This characteristic is: (a) risk-taking; (b) conformity; (c) egocentrism; (d) introversion.

7. Coping with life events is affected by all of the following except: (a) the timing of the event; (b) the family structure of the individual; (c) the personality of the individual; (d) cultural expectations for life events.

8. The sexual diamond refers to: (a) a three-year cycle that most men follow in extramarital affairs; (b) the reemergence of sexual awareness when a couple's children are grown; (c) the lifelong shifts in mood which differ for men and women; (d) the fact that sexual encounters are less frequent but more fulfilling during middle adulthood.

9. The Grant study found that men in their forties often experienced: (a) complacency about their status in life; (b) a severe devaluation of themselves; (c) a second adolescence; (d) a sense of great accomplishment and purpose.

10. Bob and Alice report that they are very happy in their marriage. They are not newly married but say they almost feel as if they were. They are most probably: (a) expecting their first child; (b) in the launching stage; (c) elderly; (d) in the process of raising a family.

PRACTICE EXERCISES

Completion

Supply the words or phrases that best complete these sentences.

1. Studies of the self-concept of adults in middle age have found that most people view themselves quite _____ in this stage.

2. Women tend to define their age status in terms of events in the _____, while men do so in terms of their _____.

3. The impulse to guide and teach the young is called _____. Those who do not develop this concern will _____, according to Erikson.

4. According tó Peck, good adjustment in midlife rests upon the development of a value of _____ rather than physical power, _____ rather than _____ in human relations, cathectic _____ rather than impoverishment, and _____ flexibility rather than rigidity.

5. In _____'s theory, people must evaluate their past in midlife and use that information to guide the future in order to develop successfully.

6. _____ has consistently been shown to increase throughout midlife.

7. The occurrence of _____ events can prove to be very difficult to cope with.

8. A time of turmoil when a person reviews his life and questions his former goals is the _____ _____. This is followed by a period of _____ when a new life structure begins to take shape.

9. The effects of health and age on happiness are such that we would expect a person to be happiest if he is _____ and _____.

10. Pineo (1961) maintains that after a long period of marriage adults often experience a drop in marital satisfaction, which he calls _____.

Matching

In the blank to the left of each definition, write the letter that indicates the term defined.

_____ 1. Concern for future generations

_____ 2. Ability to shift emotional ties

_____ 3. Ability to adjust one's thinking

_____ 4. Rebirth of storm and stress

_____ 5. Expectation of doing well

_____ 6. Triggered by a marker event

_____ 7. Period with a resurgence of marital happiness

_____ 8. Basis for early relationships in marriage

_____ 9. Gaining a realistic view of one's children

_____ 10. Possible reaction to children growing up

a. self-evaluation
b. de-illusionment
c. cathectic flexibility
d. efficacy
e. mental flexibility

f. generativity
g. empty-nest syndrome
h. attraction
i. midlife crisis
j. launching stage

True-False

Circle T if the statement is true, F if the statement is false.

T F 1. Most people in midlife rarely dwell on the fact that their friends and cohorts are beginning to die.

T F 2. The social-psychological perspective stresses adaptation to changing social situations as a dynamic force in personality functioning.

T F 3. Research in the personality of middle-agers tends to provide inconsistent findings.

T F   4.   Coping seems to be unaffected by the personality history of the individual.

T F   5.   Middle-aged men and women are often at opposite ends in their perspectives on life.

T F   6.   Data clearly indicate that a midlife crisis occurs during the early to mid-forties.

T F   7.   Layton and Siegler indicate that midlife transitions may be a crisis if efficacy is lost.

T F   8.   The happiness expressed throughout life by men and women match fairly well throughout the life span.

T F   9.   The decline in sexual expression during midlife is due to strictly cultural factors.

T F 10.   The middle aged child begins to see his parents in a more objective way and begins to see them as increasingly dependent on him.

SELF TEST B

Circle the letter of the choice that completes each item.

1. Failure to resolve the basic crises of middle adulthood, according to Erikson, will result in: (a) stagnation; (b) isolation; (c) identity diffusion; (d) generativity.

2. Four psychological developments, involving shifting values and attitudes, were seen as being important for adjustment by: (a) Maslow; (b) Buhler; (c) Peck; (d) Erikson.

3. Increased assertion is associated most closely with: (a) middle-aged men; (b) middle-aged women; (c) younger adults; (d) adolescents.

4. Improved mental health resulted for men who: (a) violated traditional sex roles; (b) were unaware of traditional sex roles; (c) adhered to traditional sex roles; (d) broke out of traditional sex roles after age 50.

5. The study of men conducted by Levinson: (a) definitely proved that there is not a midlife crisis; (b) reported a moderate midlife crisis in all men; (c) reported that a large proportion of the men had a moderate or severe crisis; (d) contradicted the notion of midlife crisis for upper-class men but not for lower and middle classes.

6. Layton and Siegler: (a) propose that midlife crisis does not exist; (b) cite efficacy as the main component of midlife crisis; (c) maintain that midlife crisis is typical of males; (d) propose that midlife crisis is brought about by fear of death.

7. The notion that midlife crisis is brought about by a series of stressful events that go beyond the individual's ability to cope is associated with: (a) Levinson; (b) Nydegger; (c) Gould; (d) Brim.

8. Happiness: (a) peaks for both men and women in midlife; (b) peaks for men in young adulthood and for women in midlife; (c) peaks for both men and women in young adulthood; (d) is lowest for men in young adulthood and for women in midlife.

9. Lucy and Harold have been married for thirty years. They still get along as well as they did at age 20 but they complain that the "fire has gone out." Pineo would say they are experiencing: (a) loss of attraction; (b) disenchantment; (c) disengagement; (d) de-illusionment.

10. A major problem for middle-aged parents is that: (a) they no longer have the energy to raise their adolescent children. (b) they can no longer remember their own adolescence and cannot understand their children's problems. (c) they can become over-identified with their children. (d) their children are changing so rapidly that parents feel even more keenly than before the burden of guiding them.

VIGNETTES

1. "I don't want to grow old!" "Never trust anyone over 30!" Statements such as these can often be heard when younger people discuss the idea of middle age. What could you say in rebuttal to these kinds of exclamations?

2. If you were working as a marriage counselor, what would you anticipate would be the most common problems you would hear from middle-aged couples?

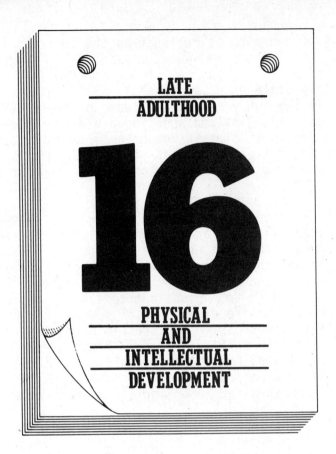

LATE
ADULTHOOD

16

PHYSICAL
AND
INTELLECTUAL
DEVELOPMENT

INTEGRATOR

In contrast to what occurs in young and middle adulthood (Chapters
12 and 14), the physical and intellectual functioning of the elderly
begins to decline noticeably. However, many of the problems in
assessing performance, particularly intellectual performance, discussed in previous chapters may be confounding that decline. If
this is true, we may be wasting a large resource by limiting the
contributions of the aged to society. One alternative proposed is
to expand the adult-education programs described in Chapter 14 to
include even older adults.

OVERVIEW

Physical Functioning

Stereotypes, mostly negative, of the old person abound in American
society. Ageism is extremely prevalent and although the science of
gerontology, the study of old people, has brought out many facts
to the contrary, prejudices continue. The impact of these attitudes
affects both the old person and the people with whom they must
interact. An increasingly large portion of the American population
is over 65. The text considers the possible causes and implications

of this graying of our population, such as the increase interest in geriatrics.

It is difficult to state exactly when "old age" begins. There is wide variation in the behavior and attitudes of individuals. Neugarten, for example, distinguishes young-old from old-old. Senescence, the period of time in which one grows old, starts at different times for different people. This period is marked by physical aging and is a better marker of old age than is chronological age.

The majority of the elderly are reasonably healthy; however, they do suffer from more illnesses and chronic health conditions than do younger populations. The text outlines some of these conditions and questions whether these stem from primary aging, an inevitable and inborn biological change, or from secondary aging, the result of trauma or chronic disease. Despite more illness and more frequent need of care, the life expectancy of today's old people is far greater than in times past. As a result of medical advances, the causes of death have shifted from childbirth and infectious disease to heart disease, cancer, and stroke. Men tend to be more vulnerable during this period; there appear to be both biological and environmental reasons for lower mortality among women.

For the most part, the sensory abilities of the aged are on the decline, with hearing impairments being the most common. Other physical and anatomical changes also take place, the most serious being those concerning the heart. Psychomotor abilities also decrease, primarily because of a slowdown in the ability to process information and react to environmental events. Physical exercise during the adult period reduces the decline in physical functioning.

Why people age is not known. Genetic factors certainly play a role as do lifelong health habits, but this does not explain how the process of aging itself works in our bodies. Numerous theories of this aging process have been presented, and the text reviews nine such theories which can be classified as either programmed process theories or as cumulative insult theories. Theories reviewed include: the gene theory, the running-out-of-program theory, somatic mutation theory, cross-linkage theory, free radical theory, clinker theory, the error theory, the wear and tear theory and the autoimmune theory. Despite the multitude of ideas, the exact nature of the aging process remains unknown.

Key terms in this section:

ageism	primary aging
graying of America	secondary aging
gerontology	programmed process theories of
geriatrics	aging
young-old vs. old-old	cumulative insult theories of
senescence	aging

Mental Health

As is true of people at any age, most old people are emotionally
healthy. It is true, however, that the elderly period presents
an unusually high incidence of stressful events with which the old
person must cope. As a result, the incidence of mental illness
among the elderly is unusually high despite the fact that most old
people are in good emotional condition. Though studies of cognitive
therapy indicate that old persons can be helped with their problems,
they are reluctant, for several reasons outlined in the text, to
seek help. Specific mental illnesses associated with elderly populations include: senility, chronic brain syndromes such as
Alzheimer's disease, intellectual impairment due to cerebral arteriosclerosis, drug intoxication, and depression.

Key terms in this section:

cognitive therapy   Alzheimer's disease
senility   cerebral arteriosclerosis
chronic brain syndrome

Intellectual Functioning in Late Adulthood

Recent research supports the contention that general intellectual
decline in old age is largely a myth. While it is true that intelligence-test performance is lower for this group, it is proposed
that this may not be a valid test of their competence. Most early
studies have been cross-sectional and have reported declines in
intelligence with age. However, problems inherent in this method,
such as the effects of cohort differences, may have masked the true
state of affairs. Several physical and psychological factors that
could also account for poor test performance by the aged are also
considered and include: neurological deterioration, physical
limitations, physiological factors, speed of processing, test
anxiety, inappropriateness of the tasks for this age group, cautiousness, self-defeating attitudes, lack of continued intellectual
activity, and terminal drop.

Studies of Piagetian abilities indicate that the aged may do less
well in conservation, may be more egocentric than younger adults
and classify in a manner similar to children. All such studies
have been cross-sectional, however, and conclusions regarding
Piagetian-type performance must remain tentative as it relates to
the aged.

Longitudinal research does not support the notion of a decline in
intellectual functioning in old age. This method, of course, also
has its limitations. The fact that the elderly may maintain their
intellectual capacity raises the question of improving this capacity
through training. Though the area is new, indications are that
training may be beneficial for the aged in improving test performance.

225

A significant aspect of intellectual functioning is the ability to learn or remember new information. The processes involved in memory are complex and involve perception, short-term storage, and long-term storage. Research has shown that older people are able to learn and remember, but they need more time to do so. It is suggested that this reflects a loss of efficiency in short-term storage. The fact that older people do as well as younger adults on recognition tasks but poorer on recall tasks indicates further that the problem may be one of retrieval rather than storage. The text then briefly considers the implications of this research for society in general and for adult training programs in particular.

Key terms in this section:

performance vs. competence	short-term storage
terminal drop	long-term storage
cross-sequential design	recognition vs. recall tasks

Work and Retirement

Retirement is a growing phenomenon in American society, and most retirees want to retire. Generally, the process preceding retirement is more stressful than the act of retiring itself. The reactions of an individual to retirement can vary widely depending upon a number of factors such as education level, financial situations, whether retirement is voluntary, and so on. As is true with all phases of life, there are both good and bad points about retirement. Gender differences also emerge in relation to adjustment to retirement though little is known about the impact of retirement upon women.

The text describes methods for making retirement a positive event by planning for it, managing leisure time, and doing away with compulsory retirement.

LEARNING OBJECTIVES

1. Define the term "ageism" and explain how it can affect the behavior and well-being of the elderly. (p. 504)

2. Define senescence and explain its major determinant. (pp. 505-506)

3. Explain what is meant by the "graying of America." (p. 505)

4. Summarize the health status of the elderly as it compares to younger segments of the population. (pp. 506-507)

5. Explain the difference between primary and secondary aging. (p. 507)

6. Discuss how the causes of death among the elderly have changed since the turn of the century and list some factors which have contributed to this shift. (pp. 507-508)

7. List several factors which contribute to the lower mortality rate amongst women in the aged population. (pp. 508-509)

8. Describe the changes that occur in the sensory capabilities of the aged. (pp. 509-510)

9. Briefly describe the major anatomical and physiological changes that occur in old age. (pp. 510-511)

10. Discuss the effects of the slowdown in information processing on the skills of the elderly. (pp. 511-512)

11. Briefly describe nine theories of the aging process. (pp. 512-514)

   a.

   b.

   c.

   d.

   e.

   f.

g.

h.

i.

12. List four physical factors and six psychological factors that might limit the performance of the elderly on intelligence tests. (pp. 520-523)

Physical

a.

b.

c.

d.

Psychological

a.

b.

c.

d.

e.

f.

13. Describe the general emotional health of the elderly and
ennumerate five specific mental-health problems of the aged.
(pp. 514-517)

General description:

Problems:

a.

b.

c.

d.

e.

14. Explain how longitudinal and cross-sectional tests of intelligence might have shortcomings and how cross-sequential designs may overcome these problems. (pp. 518-519)

15. Compare the performance of the aged to other age groups on Piagetian type tasks. (pp. 519-520)

16. Point out the distinction between short-term and long-term memory and explain how the abilities of the elderly compare with those of other groups on these two types of memory. (pp. 524-525)

17. Describe how memory loss in the aged is related to efficiency of short-term storage, organization of material, and retrieval of information. (pp. 524-526)

18. Describe the reactions of the elderly to retirement, and list factors which are associated with these reactions. (pp. 527-528)

19. Describe three steps that can be used to make retirement a positive experience. (p. 529)

   a.

   b.

   c.

SELF TEST A

Circle the letter of the choice that completes each item.

1. The scientific study of the process of aging is called:

(a) ageism; (b) geriatrics; (c) gerontology; (d) terminal psychology.

2. Larry is experiencing significant physical decline. He has just turned 70 and has had two mild strokes. In addition, his gastrointestinal tract has an infection and he has developed a muscle spasm in his left leg. We would say that Larry has entered: (a) terminal drop; (b) a climacteric; (c) senescence; (d) senility.

3. Aging that is due to trauma or disease is called: (a) primary aging; (b) secondary aging; (c) gerontological aging; (d) traumatic senescence.

4. Women tend to live longer than men because: (a) they have greater natural immunity to disease; (b) of genetic factors; (c) of different lifestyles; (d) of both environmental and genetic factors.

5. Peter is 78 years old. We would expect to find his greatest sensory deficit in the sense of: (a) vision; (b) hearing; (c) taste; (d) smell.

6. The most serious physiological changes in aging are those affecting the: (a) heart; (b) bones; (c) brain; (d) eyes.

7. That aging is due to limited amounts of available genetic material is the central concept of the: (a) gene theory of aging; (b) cross-linkage theory of aging; (c) running-out-of-program theory of aging; (d) error theory of aging.

8. Irreversible mental and physical deterioration associated with aging is called: (a) chronic brain syndrome; (b) senility; (c) arteriosclerosis; (d) Alzheimer's disease.

9. Which of the following is true regarding the performance of the elderly on intelligence tests? (a) Those who engage in physical activity do better on these tests. (b) They tend to be less cautious and more confident. (c) They are usually highly motivated and interested in taking the test. (d) They use the same problem-solving techniques as do younger people.

10. Elderly subjects do <u>least</u> well on tasks: (a) with a speed requirement; (b) that tap vocabulary skills; (c) that are familiar; (d) that tap long-term memory.

PRACTICE EXERCISES

<u>Completion</u>

Supply the words or phrases that best complete these sentences.

1. Most of the stereotypes about the aged are _____, and although many of them are false, this prejudice against the elderly, or _____, can have serious effects on the individual.

2. _____ is the study of the elderly and the process of aging. This is an important endeavor because the number of old people in our society is _____.

3. Neugarten (1968) makes a distinction between the "_____ - _____" on the basis of activity level and social participation.

4. The portion of the life span during which one grows old is _____. The major sign of its onset is _____ aging.

5. Innate biological changes produce _____ aging, while trauma and disease are responsible for _____ aging.

6. The death rate in the United States has been _____ rapidly, but the leading causes of death have shifted with _____, _____, and _____ becoming more important.

7. One possible reason for the high accident rate among the elderly might be the _____ in information processing.

8. The _____ theory of aging says that the structure of DNA changes with age, resulting in the production of defective enzymes.

9. A sudden decline in intellectual performance prior to death is called _____ _____.

10. Studies show that _____ memory abilities decline with age, while _____ memory abilities do not.

Matching

In the blank to the left of each definition, write the letter that indicates the term defined.

_____ 1. Common health problem of the aged

_____ 2. Caused shifts in cause of death in U.S. elderly

_____ 3. Anatomical change after menopause

_____ 4. Inherited aging theory

_____ 5. Aging due to altered proteins

_____ 6. Aging due to enzymes

_____ 7. Condition which can cause intellectual impairment

_____ 8. Combines longitudinal and cross-sectional techniques

_____ 9. Lowers intelligence-test performance of elderly

_____ 10. Memory for recent material

_____ 11. Memory skill fairly stable in aged

_____ 12. Piagetian task in which aged do less well

a. sanitation, immunization
b. cerebral arteriosclerosis
c. gene theory
d. cross-linkage theory
e. short-term
f. long-term
g. widow's hump
h. chronic conditions
i. error theory
j. conservation
k. speed, attitude, and cautiousness
l. cross-sequential

Word Scrambler

Unscramble the ten items. Then arrange the circled letters to complete the sentence below.

1. _ _ O _ _ O
   G M A S E I
   Prejudice against the elderly

2. _ _ O _ _ _ _ _ . _ _ _
   E Y T O L G O R N O G
   Study of aging

3. _ _ _ _ _ O _ _ _ _
   I T E R G A R C S I
   Medical treatment of the aged

236

4. _ _ Ⓞ _ _ _ _ _ _ _
   E N C S E S N E C E
   Period in which one grows old

5. Ⓞ _ _ _ _ _ _
   R A Y M R I P
   Aging due to inborn program

6. _ _ _ _ _ _ Ⓞ _ _ _
   N E C A S Y R O D
   Aging due to disease

7. _ _ _ _ _ _ Ⓞ _ _
   N I S T Y L I E
   Irreversible deterioration of aged

8. Ⓞ _ _ _ _ _ _ _ _ 's
   E L Z I A M E H R
   Disease which is chronic brain syndrome

9. _ Ⓞ _ _ _ _ _ _ _ _
   E O T E M N C C E P
   Underlying ability

10. _ Ⓞ _ _ - _ _ _ _ _ _ _ _ _ Ⓞ
    S R O C S L U Q T E S N A E I
    Research design combining two others

    Just before death, many individuals exhibit a sudden decline

    in functioning known as _ _ _ _ _ _ _ _

    _ _ _ _.

SELF TEST B

Circle the letter of the choice that completes each item.

1. The elderly generally have: (a) fewer colds and flu infections than younger people; (b) more colds and flu infections than younger people; (c) a lower rate of chronic disease than younger people; (d) about the same level of motor skill as younger people.

2. The "graying of America" refers to a: (a) steady increase in ageism over the past three decades; (b) steady increase in the size of the elderly population; (c) greater tendency on the part of the elderly to speak out in their own behalf; (d) trend toward early retirement in American society.

3. Alfred has been sick for almost all of the past 15 years. He is now 65 and is very frail and suffers many ailments. Alfred has experienced: (a) senility; (b) primary aging; (c) secondary aging; (d) terminal drop.

4. The error theory of aging maintains that: (a) the immunological system functions differently; (b) cells can divide only a finite number of times; (c) defective enzymes are produced by changes in DNA; (d) bad genes become dominate in later life.

5. Most early cross-sectional studies of intelligence in old age: (a) showed steady increments in IQ; (b) combined different abilities that could mask developmental trends; (c) are still valid today; (d) were able to overcome the problem of cohort effects.

6. The sudden drop in intellectual performance shortly before death is called: (a) ageism; (b) senescence; (c) terminal drop; (d) senility.

7. Cross-sequential studies of intelligence have found that differences between cohorts were: (a) nearly nonexistent; (b) similar to age changes for given individuals; (c) smaller than age changes for given individuals; (d) larger than age changes for given individuals.

8. Older people learn best when: (a) material is presented slowly; (b) the task involves short-term memory; (c) the task requires recall; (d) the task ignores accuracy.

9. It has been reported that elderly subjects: (a) may have trouble in organizing information to be remembered; (b) organize information as well as younger subjects do; (c) organize information better than younger subjects do; (d) do not attempt to organize information before storing it.

10. Retirement can best be made a positive experience by: (a) making it totally compulsory; (b) avoiding making plans until after retiring; (c) learning to use leisure time wisely; (d) anticipating a decline in physical health after retirement.

VIGNETTES

Give yourself and some of your friends the following short quiz.

Answer True or False:

1. Old people spend most of their time in bed because of illness.
2. Old people tend to have many accidents in the home.
3. Old people are less intelligent than when they were younger.
4. Old people have poor memories.

5. Old people have little interest in sexual relationships.
6. Most old people do little work that is productive.
7. Old people are grouchy.
8. Old people do not really want to retire.
9. Most old people live in nursing homes or institutions.
10. Old people cannot learn new information as well as young people can.

To what extent are your answers, and those of your friends, in line with the stereotypes?

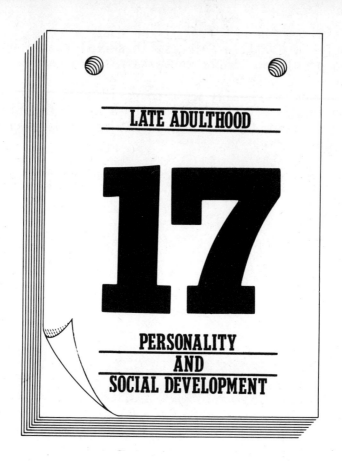

LATE ADULTHOOD

17

**PERSONALITY
AND
SOCIAL DEVELOPMENT**

INTEGRATOR

Personality development in old age is in many ways a continuation
of patterns of adjustment established earlier in life. In addition, there are situations peculiar to old age that require making
adjustment during this period; for example, the role of grandparent,
the loss of a loved one, and societal factors such as low fixed
income and ageism. Yet, adjustment to these situations is very
much determined by basic personality patterns established over the
entire life span. Thus, old age marks the culmination of a lifetime of growth and development reviewed in preceding chapters. The
theories of Erikson, Buhler, and Peck will again be considered as
we examine this last life period. As we did in earlier chapters,
we will focus on the role of family relations and friendships and
consider the impact these may have on the individual.

OVERVIEW

Successful Aging

The view of the elderly held by American society is very negative.
The opinions and stereotypes develop very early and make successful
aging a very difficult goal to achieve. Nonetheless it is

attainable, and many aged individuals lead fruitful and fulfilling lives. Three major theories are considered which attempt to explain the process of successful aging.

One major view is that of activity theory. The general concept is that the more active an old person remains, the more successfully he or she will age. Activity can be classified as informal, formal, and solitary. Researchers have investigated each of these types but have found that activity, in and of itself, is not related to reported life satisfaction. Disengagement theory has been proposed as an alternative. This perspective defines successful aging as a mutual withdrawal of the aged person from the mainstream of life. Critics claim that this theory relates more to problems of old age than to success in aging and that it is dangerous because it justifies society's desire to ignore the elderly. The newest orientation to successful aging is offered as the social breakdown syndrome theory. This view maintains that problems in aging arise from a conflict between society's expectations for the aged and the self-concept of the aged individual. A three-step process which comprises the social reconstruction syndrome is proposed to alleviate this conflict.

Empirical research on aging has indicated that successful aging has more to do with the personality traits of the individual than it does with activity or disengagement. For example, Reichard, Livson, and Peterson have identified five patterns of aging. Three of these, the mature, the rocking-chair men, and the armored, were successful patterns, while two other patterns, the angry and the self-haters, were unsuccessful. Similarly Neugarten, Havighurst, and Tobin have identified four personality types which vary in life satisfaction. These are: integrated personalities, which include reorganizers and focused and disengaged individuals; armored-defended personalities, which include holding-on and constricted individuals; passive-dependent personalities, which include succorance-seeking and apathetic individuals; and the unintegrated personalities. Each of these patterns and individuals included within each class vary in life satisfaction.

Key terms in this section:

activity theory	self-hater personality
disengagement theory	integrated personalities
formal activity	reorganizers
informal activity	focused individuals
solitary activity	disengaged individuals
social breakdown syndrome	armored-defended personality
social reconstruction syndrome	holding-on pattern
successful aging	constricted pattern
mature personality	passive-dependent personality
rocking-chair men	succorance-seeking individual
armored personality	apathetic individual
angry personality	unintegrated personality

Personality Change and Happiness in Late Adulthood

Certain personality traits, such as rigidity, restraint, cautiousness, passivity, and concern with self, have been reported for the
aged population. The text considers the adaptive value of these
characteristics very briefly and then turns attention to the topic
of happiness. Self-esteem is a major component of happiness at
any age. Feelings of competency, control over one's life, and
access to privacy are listed as important to self-esteem for the
elderly. General life satisfaction is also affected by more-
concrete factors, with health and income being primary. There are
also sex differences, with income and education being more important
to life satisfaction for men.

Theoretical Perspectives on Aging

The next section completes the three major theories of personality
development presented in earlier chapters. The focus of Erikson's
theory is the resolution of the crisis between ego integrity versus
despair. Peck expanded upon this notion to include the resolution
between three crises: (a) ego-differentiation versus work-role
preoccupation, (b) body transcendence versus body preoccupation,
and (c) ego-transcendence versus ego-preoccupation. Buhler's emphasis is on the importance of developing a sense of totality of
one's life. All three of these theories share the emphasis on life
review and a focus on a re-evaluation of one's life.

Key terms in this section:

ego integrity vs. despair
ego-differentiation vs. work-
    role preoccupation

body transcendence vs. body
    preoccupation
ego-transcendence vs. ego-
    preoccupation

Aging and the Family

Marriages between the elderly are typically more enjoyable and
happier than with younger couples. The text considers several
reasons for the high level of marital satisfaction during this
period and notes that marriage is an important component of morale
for both men and women although for different reasons. Remarriage
during the later years is an increasing phenomenon and the text
considers a number of reasons people give for remarrying. The benefits of remarriage for the individual and society are potentially
substantial.

Despite the stereotypes of the elderly as sexless, sexual activity
can and should play an important role during the later years. Main-
taining an active sex life throughout adulthood is the best way to
provide for sexual capacity in old age. While sex is present
during the elderly period, it is different and the text reviews

some of the differences. Men and women report different sexual interests; this reflects biological differences as well as the sexual double-standard in American culture.

Widowhood is the hardest burden to bear during old age. More often the male dies first and women over 65 outnumber men by 3 million. The text considers the impact of the loss of a spouse on the individual and his or her daily life. People who never marry seem to be less affected by old age, which may reflect different life experiences or personalities.

Contrary to popular belief, the vast majority of the elderly report being satisfied with the way they interrelate with their families. There are specific differences, however, with noninstitutionalized and old-old individuals reporting more satisfaction with family relations than young-old and instituionalized elderly. The role of parent for the elderly is a complex one. The text considers several factors which contribute to this complexity such as shifts in helping with grandparents getting more help than they give, strivings for independence by adult children, and current lifestyles in which parents and children do not share the same household. In addition to the role of parent, the elderly must also adjust to a new social role, grandparenting. Several styles of grandparenting have been delineated. These are: the formal grandparent, the fun seeker, the surrogate parent, the reservoir of family wisdom, and the distant figure. The fun seeker and distant figure are the most-often used, but style is primarily an individual factor. Children's preferences for grandparents are also considered.

The importance of close personal relationships is briefly considered. The existence of a companion, a confidant, and a sympathetic listener can have definite benefits for the elderly person.

Key terms in this section:

formal grandparent	reservoir of family wisdom
fun seeker	distant figure
surrogate parent	

Some Social Issues Related to Aging

Friendships have been found to be an important component of life at all stages of development, and the later years are no exception. Older people tend to choose their friends on much the same basis as do younger adults with similarity and proximity being the leading factors. The text considers the impact of changes in status, such as early retirement, social class, and sex differences, on the role of friendships for the elderly. In general, friends can offer much, especially emotional support, when family members are not sufficiently available.

Income is probably the biggest problem facing the elderly. Poverty
is inordinately common for those over 65. The text describes some
steps that may help to solve this problem. Inadequate housing is
a related problem. Contrary to popular stereotypes, only a small
portion of the elderly population live in institutions. Keeping
the elderly in the community; the impact, both positive and negative, of institutionalization; and the problem of crime and the
elderly are also considered by the text.

Cross-cultural Patterns of Aging

Cross-cultural studies of aging give us some clues about the factors
that are associated with longevity and also give us information on
differing patterns of adjustment. In general, minority groups in
America seem to suffer many of the negative consequences of aging
in addition to those associated with racial prejudice. These elderly often find themselves in a multiple-jeopardy situation. In
other cultures, differing from ours primarily in diet and level of
exercise and where societal attitudes differ toward aging, the
process can have a more positive aspect.

LEARNING OBJECTIVES

1. Describe the general attitudes of American society toward the
    elderly and trace the development of these attitudes in
    children. (p. 536)

2. Describe the activity theory of successful aging and in the
    process differentiate among informal, formal, and solitary
    activity and note whether or not research has supported this
    theory. (p. 538)

3. Describe the disengagement theory of successful aging and note whether or not research has supported this theory. (p. 538)

4. Define "social breakdown syndrome." (p. 539)

5. List three steps which make up social reconstruction syndrome. (p. 539)

   a.

   b.

   c.

6. Name and describe the five patterns of aging proposed by Reichard, Levson and Peterson and identify each as successful or unsuccessful. (pp. 539-540)

   a.

   b.

c.

d.

e.

7. Name four personality types proposed by Neugarten, Havighurst, and Tobin and describe the types of individuals included in each type of personality with special emphasis on the level of life satisfaction associated with each type of person. (pp. 540-541)

   a. Personality type:

      Individuals 1.

                  2.

                  3.

   b. Personality type:

Individuals 1.

2.

c. Personality type:

Individuals 1.

2.

d. Personality type:

8. Describe how the circumstances surrounding old age can contribute to a loss of self-esteem and what can be done to improve self-esteem. (pp. 541-542)

9. Describe the events which characterize Erikson's last stage of
personality development. (p. 543)

10. Summarize Peck's three stages of psychological development in old age. (pp. 543-544)

a.

b.

c.

11. List the events which Buhler proposes are involved in the last stage of psychological growth. (pp. 544-545)

12. Describe the level of satisfaction with and the functions of marriage in the old age period. (pp. 545-547)

13. Explain why the elderly might remarry and describe the possible benefits of remarriage at this stage of development. (pp. 547-548)

14. Describe how sexuality is different during the elderly period and list those factors which contribute to these differences for men and women. (pp. 548-550)

15. Describe the impact of widowhood on the individual. (pp. 550-552)

16. Describe the typical attitudes of the elderly toward their families and discuss some factors which are related to these attitudes. (p. 552)

17. Briefly discuss why parenthood is a complex role for the
    elderly. (pp. 553-554)

18. List and briefly describe five major styles of grandparenting.
    (pp. 554-555)

    a.

    b.

    c.

    d.

    e.

19. Explain why close personal relationships are important in
    old age. (pp. 555-556)

20. Discuss the following five problems as they are commonly asso-
    ciated with the lifestyles of the elderly. (pp. 558-562)

    Income:

    Housing:

    Community involvement:

    Institutionalization:

    Crime:

21. Describe the impact of each of the following on friendship
    patterns in the elderly and discuss the function of friend-
    ships in this period. (pp. 556-557)

Change of status

Social class

Sex differences

Function of friendship

22. Describe the multiple jeopardy of the minority group elderly. (pp. 562-563)

23. Describe the factors which seem to be associated with longevity in other cultures. (pp. 563-564)

SELF TEST A

Circle the letter of the choice that completes each item.

1. Stereotypes of the elderly tend to develop during: (a) middle adulthood, as the period of old age approaches; (b) adolescence, with the advent of formal operations; (c) early childhood and then persist throughout the lifespan; (d) the infancy period and are well established as early as the preschool years.

2. Successful aging seems most closely related to: (a) gender; (b) self-esteem; (c) activity level; (d) early retirement.

3. Remaining in as many organizations and groups as possible and keeping busy is the key to successful aging according to: (a) activity theory; (b) disengagement theory; (c) mainstream-of-life theory; (d) identity theory.

4. According to social reconstruction theory, to bring about successful aging we should: (a) emphasize exactly what society expects the old person to do; (b) provide social services to the elderly; (c) provide more guidelines and directions for the elderly; (d) leave control of the elderly population to the direction of the department of social services.

5. Two groups of people who have been shown to experience unsuccessful patterns of aging are: (a) angry men and self-haters; (b) angry men and rocking-chair men; (c) armored men and self-haters; (d) self-haters and mature men.

6. Doug is an elderly gentleman who is very active. He cannot do the things he used to do but he has replaced many old activities with new ones which he enjoys. Doug is best classified as: (a) focused; (b) disengaged; (c) holding-on; (d) reorganizer.

7. Willard is 71 years old. He is best described as striving, achievement-oriented, and tightly controlled. He has dealt with old age by doing as much of the things he used to do as possible. Willard is best classified as a(n): (a) integrated personality; (b) passive-dependent personality; (c) armored-defended personality; (d) unintegrated personality.

8. In Peck's theory, the failure to redefine one's worth beyond one's vocation is called: (a) ego-differentiation; (b) ego-preoccupation; (c) work-role preoccupation; (d) ego-transcendence.

9. Marriages in the elderly period tend to be: (a) happier than those in other life periods; (b) very rare; (c) void of sexual component; (d) less satisfying than in other life periods.

10. Multiple jeopardy is a term used to describe the combined

negative effects of being: (a) poor and blind; (b) old and poor; (c) old and alone; (d) old and a minority.

Completion

Supply the words or phrases that best complete these sentences.

1. For many elderly, the negative stereotypes of the elderly person and loss of control over their own lives results in a

   loss of _____.

2. Remaining active is the key to successful aging, according to

   the _____ theory of aging. _____
   theory views normal aging as the mutual withdrawal of the
   elderly and society.

3. One study by Reichard et al. has shown that people who best adjusted to growing old were those who were classified as

   _____, _____, or as _____-

   _____ men.

4. The Kansas City study of adult life found that people with well-adjusted, integrated personalities fell into three groups:

   the _____, the _____, and the

   _____. All these groups adjusted well to old

   age. In contrast, people with _____ personalities showed a negative pattern of adjustment.

5. According to Erikson, good adjustment in old age revolves around the acceptance of one's past life and impending death,

   or _____. Failure to accomplish this results

   in _____.

6. In Peck's theory, people who realize that their accomplishments have enduring significance are said to achieve

   _____. Similarly, those who are less
   preoccupied with their physical decline and focus on personal

   relationships have achieved _____.

7. Widowhood is more prevalent among _____ than

   _____, primarily because of the former living
   longer.

8. A grandparent who assumes a major role in taking care of the

   grandchildren is playing a _____ parent role. People
   who have only occasional contact with their grandchildren are

   said to be _____ figures.

9. The biggest problem affecting old people in our society is

   _____.

10. The problems associated with aging in our society seem to be

    even more pronounced for members of _____
    groups. For example, minority group members are less likely

    to be covered by _____ benefits, since
    they frequently die before they can collect them.

True-False

Circle T if the statement is true, F if the statement is false.

T F   1. Research data have strongly supported the activity and
         disengagement theories of aging.

T F   2. Eliminating ageism, providing social services for the
         elderly, and giving them control over their lives is
         the social reconstruction syndrome.

T F   3. Armored-defended personalities are found to have very
         low life satisfaction.

T F   4. Being able to ignore physical decline of aging to some
         extent will greatly improve a person's body trans-
         cendence.

T F   5. According to Buhler, seeing one's life as a totality is
         central to successful aging.

T F   6. Marriages in late adulthood tend to be unhappy and are
         best classified as passive-congenial.

T F   7. Remarriage in late adulthood is almost always a bad
         idea, as older persons have difficulty adjusting to
         married life.

T F   8. Differences in the interest level and practice of
         sexuality between men and women is due to our sexual

255

double standard and not to biological differences.

T F   9.   Gaining a strong sense of one's own identity is the best preparation for eventual widowhood.

T F 10.   People who have never married tend to be better adjusted to old age.

T F 11.   During late adulthood, patterns of helping shift and elderly parents usually get more help than they receive.

T F 12.   Elderly parents and middle-age children rarely share the same household today and as a result see each other only rarely.

T F 13.   The authoritarian grandparent role is called the resevoir of family wisdom style.

T F 14.   Women tend to have closer friendships than men do in old age.

T F 15.   Federal-government surveys reveal that the housing owned by old people is significantly worse than that owned by younger adults.

Word Scrambler

Unscramble the ten items. Then arrange the circled letters to complete the sentence below.

1. _ _ _ _ _ _ _ _
   I V I A T C Y T
   Theory of aging stressing keeping busy

2. Ⓞ _ _ _ _ _ _ _
   I O L R A Y S T
   Activity not involving others

3. _ _ Ⓞ _ _ _ _ _ _
   R D B A K N E W O
   When self-image and society conflict, it is called social
   _ _ _ _ _ _.

4. _ _ _ _ _ Ⓞ _ _ _
   P E H T A C T I A
   People who have been passive all their lives

256

5. ___ ___ Ⓞ ___ ___ ___ ___
   P   A   R   D   I   E   S
Negative outcome in Erikson's last stage

6. ___ ___ ___ -
   G   O   E

 ___ ___ ___ Ⓞ ___ ___ ___ ___ ___ ___ ___ ___ ___ ___
   T   I   F   E   O   I   N   F   I   N   D   A   E   T   R
Redefining oneself outside of vocation

7. ___ ___ ___ Ⓞ ___ ___ ___ ___ ___ ___ ___
   E   N   D   E   N   E   I   C   N   P   E   D
Striving for this by adult children can make the parent role complex for the elderly

8. ___ ___ ___ ___ ___ Ⓞ
   A   L   O   F   M   R
Grandparents who do not raise grandchildren; give some gifts and babysit

9. ___ ___ ___ Ⓞ ___ ___ ___
   Y   O   V   P   R   E   T
Number one problem of elderly

10. ___ ___ ___ Ⓞ ___ ___ ___ Ⓞ ___
   M   T   O   N   Y   C   I   U   M
Where most old people live

A major component of successful aging is to have high

___ ___ ___ ___ - ___ ___ ___ ___ ___ ___ ___.

SELF TEST B

Circle the letter of the choice that completes each item.

1. An important aspect of successful aging is the: (a) degree of activity one maintains; (b) amount of involvement one has in social interactions; (c) personality traits and habits that have characterized one's entire life; (d) closeness one has to other family members.

2. People who hold on as long as possible to patterns of middle age are said to be: (a) armored-defensive; (b) passive-dependent; (c) unintegrated; (d) integrated.

3. In Erikson's theory, people who fail to accept their lives and impending death suffer: (a) ego-differentiation; (b) ego-preoccupation; (c) despair; (d) ego-transcendence.

4. Buhler has found that in old age, most people experience: (a) despair and depression; (b) a sense of total fulfillment; (c) partial fulfillment and some disappointments; (d) a sense of loss and panic over so little time left.

5. Remarriage in the elderly period is most often for the purpose of: (a) relieving loneliness; (b) bolstering one's financial situation; (c) gaining sexual outlet; (d) attracting the attention and social outlets of others.

6. Research data indicate that in the elderly period: (a) men remain more sexually active than women; (b) women remain more sexually active than men; (c) men and women remain equally active sexually; (d) both men and women stop having sexual relations by age 60.

7. The grandparent who plays the role of playmate to the grandchildren is called a: (a) surrogate parent; (b) reservoir of family wisdom; (c) fun seeker; (d) distant person.

8. Most old people live in: (a) some kind of institution; (b) the community, alone or with their relatives or friends; (c) their children's homes; (d) special apartments and government housing.

9. Personal change in response to becoming widowed is least likely for women who: (a) didn't get along with their husbands; (b) are less educated; (c) are more active socially; (d) are better off financially.

10. The major problem of the elderly in America today is: (a) institutionalization; (b) housing; (c) crime; (d) poverty.

VIGNETTE

1. Your roommate says that she is concerned because her recently retired grandparents don't _do_ anything. They never were overly active but your roommate feels that they should get out now, meet people, and have a good time. How might you respond?

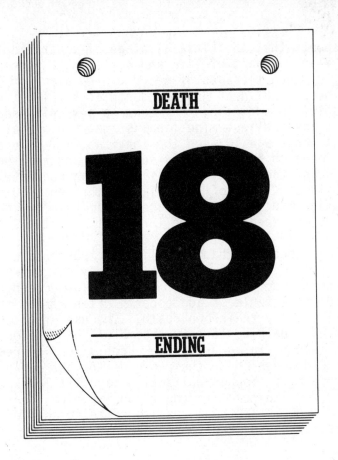

DEATH

18

ENDING

INTEGRATOR

In the previous 17 chapters, numerous stages of development, challenges, and major life events were described. Chapter 18 deals with the last major event in the life span--death. Once again we will see that people vary greatly in their reactions to their own death and to the death of others. In general, however, adjustment to death will be seen to depend upon what has gone before in a person's life. Therefore, all that we have learned about human development in Chapters 1 through 17 has relevance for this topic.

OVERVIEW

Attitudes Toward Death Across the Life Span

American culture has dealth with death by attempting to prolong life through medical advancement and thereby push death out of the collective awareness of society. Recently, the new science of death, thanatology, has promoted a healthier view and new awareness of the importance of death as a developmental stage.

At ages 2 and 3, children have no idea what death means. Nagy has studied the development of a concept of death through the childhood period and reports that this initial stage of separation, in which children see death as part of life and something reversible, lasts until age 5. Between the ages of 5 and 9, the stage of personification takes over. Children now see death as final but do not see it as inevitable; in addition, they tend to personify death, as the name of this stage implies. The final stage, biological universal, is achieved at about age 10 when the inevitability of death is understood. Research has variously supported and refuted this progression, and the stages outlined may not be appropriate for all children. Children dying of leukemia go through a quite different sequence of stages in their understanding of their own death. The five stages are outlined in Figure 18-1 in the text.

Adolescents have generally had very little experience with death and approach this topic with the same wide variety of reactions that typify their approach to other topics. The egocentrism, denial, and personal fable in adolescents often affect their views on death, particularly their own death. The use of black humor is often effective in helping to defuse some of the tension surrounding the death issue. In general, adolescents tend to react with anger more than depression to their own death, but denial is the most common response. Young adults also have little experience with death and tend to react to their own impending death with great anger. There is a strong feeling of being cheated out of the life they have worked so hard to prepare for.

In middle age, a number of factors contribute to a "true realization" of the certainty of death. This realization precipitates numerous responses such as a shift in time orientation, initiation of the life review, and possibly major life readjustments.

The elderly, in general, are less likely to be anxious about death. Being cut off from the mainstream of life and a history of chronic physical ailments can, in some instances, make death seem like a reasonable alternative. Finding purpose in one's life, and death, can be a critical factor in adjustment to death.

Key terms in this section:

thanatology
separation stage
personification stage

biological universal stage
black humor

Suicide and Death Education

Suicide among 15- to 24-year-olds has increased at an alarming rate since 1968. The text considers possible reasons why young people try and sometimes succeed in killing themselves. Social isolation, behavior problems, delinquency, mental and family problems are all among the possible factors contributing to adolescent suicide. In college populations, social isolation seems to be an important

variable. Pressures from the need to do well in school do not seem
to be a major factor.

Amongst the elderly, sucide is an especially prevalent problem. A
deep sense of loss is often associated with suicide for the elderly.
Specific sex and race effects are also seen in the incidence of
suicide during late adulthood. Education about death is increasing
and can be very useful in helping individuals adjust to death. The
text outlines some of the important aims of death-education programs.

Facing Death

The stages that people pass through in accepting their own death
have been outlined by Kübler-Ross (1969). She proposed that there
are five such stages: denial, anger, bargaining, depression, and
ultimate acceptance. These stages are not inevitable for all dying
patients and are intended only as a useful guideline.

Another interesting conceptualization is proposed by Pattison. He
proposes that significant changes in a person's trajectory of life
occur during the living-dying interval as a result of the pronouncement of a person's impending death. The living-dying interval is
comprised of an acute phase, a chronic living-dying phase, and a
terminal phase. Numerous dying trajectories are possible, and the
text considers four of these. In addition, four types of death,
sociological, psychic, biological, and physiological, are defined.

Psychological changes which occur during the terminal drop period
are described and a total system decline is suggested. The role of
the life review is considered in the final portion of this section.

Key terms in this section:

denial   chronic living-dying phase
anger   terminal phase
depression   dying trajectory
bargaining   sociological death
ultimate acceptance   psychic death
trajectory of life   biological death
living-dying interval   physiological death
acute phase   total system decline

Ethical Issues and Ways to Help Terminal Patients

Numerous ethical issues are associated with the topic of death.
Various ethical questions are raised in this section for which
there are no simple answers. Euthanasia, whether active or passive,
is a well-known example of such complex ethical issues.

The special needs of the terminally ill are better met in special
institutions, called hospices, than in hospitals which are

oriented to making people get better. <u>Make Today Count</u> and <u>Shanti Project</u> describe other attempts to meet the special needs of terminal patients.

Key terms in this section:

euthanasia	hospice
passive euthanasia	Make Today Count
active euthanasia	the Shanti Project

Bereavement, Mourning, and Grief

The absence of universal mourning rites in America can pose a major problem to the survivors who lose a loved one. The status of bereavement often has associated with it a specific set of behaviors referred to as mourning. These behaviors are poorly defined in American culture and are less effective in helping the person express the emotional impact of his or her loss, called grief. Grief can be of several forms, including: anticipatory grief, normal grief, and morbid grief. Normal grief is further broken down into three stages: the initial phase, the intermediate phase, and the recovery phase. While it is not always required, grief therapy is available from a number of sources.

Key terms in this section:

bereavement	anticipatory grief
mourning	morbid grief
grief	normal grief

LEARNING OBJECTIVES

1. Briefly describe how American society has dealth with death and how the science of thanatology is affecting these attitudes. (p. 570)

2. Describe Nagy's three stages in children's development of a death concept.   (p. 571)

   a.

   b.

   c.

3. Review the research relating to the accuracy of Nagy's proposed developmental progression.   (pp. 571-572)

4. Describe the five stages in the thinking about death exhibited by children who are victims of leukemia.   (p. 573)

   a.

   b.

c.

d.

e.

5. Describe the reactions to death in individuals in each of the following age groups: (pp. 574-577)

    Adolescence:

    Young adults:

    Middle-aged adults:

    The elderly:

6. Describe the importance of "finding purpose in one's life" to the adjustment to death. (pp. 577-578)

7. List several factors which contribute to suicide in adolescence. (pp. 578-580)

8. Describe significant factors which contribute to suicide in young adults and in the elderly. (p. 580)

Young adults:

The elderly:

9. List some important aims in death education. (p. 581)

10. List and describe five stages in facing one's own death proposed by Kübler-Ross. (pp. 582-583)

   a.

   b.

   c.

   d.

   e.

11. Define each of the following concepts. (pp. 584-585)

   Trajectory of life:

   Living-dying interval:

   Dying trajectory:

12. List and describe the three phases of Pattison's living-dying interval. (p. 584)

a.

b.

c.

13. Name four dying trajectories. (p. 585)

a.

b.

c.

d.

14. Describe the type of death being referenced by each of the following terms. (p. 585)

Sociological death:

Psychic death:

Biological death:

Physiological death:

15. Explain what is meant by the term "total system decline."
    (p. 585)

16. Discuss the role of the life review in adjusting to death.
    (p. 586)

17. Differentiate between active and passive euthanasia. (p. 588)

18. Describe how each of the following helps to meet the special needs of the terminal patient. (pp. 588-591)

    Hospice:

    Make Today Count:

    Shanti Project:

19. Differentiate among the concepts: bereavement, mourning, and grief. (pp. 591-592)

20. List and describe three types of grief. (pp. 592-593)

    a.

b.

c.

21. List and describe three phases of normal grief. (pp. 592-593)

a.

b.

c.

22. Briefly describe the goals and process of grief therapy.
(pp. 593-594)

SELF TEST A

Circle the letter of the choice that completes each item.

1. The study of death and dying is called: (a) morbid psychology;

(b) thanatology; (c) grief therapy; (d) terminal psychology.

2. Research with children has shown that: (a) all children understand the inevitability but not the finality of death by the age
of 5; (b) children always personify death while adults seldom do;
(c) the idea of reincarnation is common amongst children; (d) Nagy's
proposed stages are correct for all children.

3. Adolescents tend to react to information about their impending
death with: (a) denial; (b) suicide attempts; (c) depression;
(d) confusion.

4. Among adolescent populations, suicide is most often linked to:
(a) sexual problems; (b) personality disorders; (c) violence in the
media; (d) social isolation.

5. Jack is dying. He spends much of his time praying for just
enough time to see his 17-year-old daughter get married. He swears
that if he can just have that, he will be the best man on earth
for his remaining time. According to Kübler-Ross, Jack is in what
stage in accepting his death? (a) denial; (b) depression; (c)
anger; (d) bargaining.

6. A person faces the pronouncement of certain death in the near
future during the stage Pattison calls the: (a) active phase of the
living-dying interval; (b) chronic living-dying phase of the living-
dying interval; (c) terminal phase of the living-dying interval;
(d) dying trajectory.

7. John was born yesterday with a major heart defect and massive
brain malformation. It is certain that John will never be able to
care for even his most basic needs. In addition, John must have
heart surgery or it is very doubtful that he will live for more
than a few months. John's parents refuse to give permission for the
surgery feeling that John is better off dead than being a living but
helpless organism. John's parents are practicing: (a) active
euthanasia; (b) passive euthanasia; (c) death therapy; (d) thanatology.

8. The status of being without a recently deceased person is
called: (a) bereavement; (b) mourning; (c) grief; (d) morbid grief.

9. Immediately after the death of his wife, Paul was unable to
function and could not even show his feelings well. He seemed con-
fused and numb. Paul was in: (a) a state of morbid grief; (b) the
initial phase of normal grief; (c) the recovery phase of normal
grief; (d) the intermediate phase of normal grief.

10. Adjustment to death is positively correlated with: (a) finding
purpose in one's life; (b) socioeconomic standing; (c) low self-
esteem; (d) institutionalization.

PRACTICE EXERCISES

Matching

In the blank to the left of each definition, write the letter that indicates the term defined.

_____ 1. Nagy's last stage in children's development of a death concept

_____ 2. The study of death and dying

_____ 3. Used to defuse anxiety about death

_____ 4. First reaction to one's own death, according to Kübler-Ross

_____ 5. Kübler-Ross's fourth stage of accepting one's death

_____ 6. The course of dying

_____ 7. Used to aid those dealing with death

_____ 8. A predeath change in cognitive and emotional behaviors

_____ 9. Mercy-killing

_____ 10. Last stage of normal grief

a. depression
b. denial
c. recovery
d. thanatology
e. total system decline
f. euthanasia
g. biological universal
h. Shanti project
i. dying trajectory
j. black humor

True-False

Circle T if the statement is true, F if the statement is false.

T F 1. American society tends to deal with death in a "denial" fashion.

T F 2. According to Nagy, children personify death when they are about the age of 9.

T F 3. Research has strongly supported Nagy's theory.

T F 4. Young adults tend to react to death with anger.

T F 5. The elderly, because it is much closer, are most anxious about death.

T F 6. Suicide is related to a sense of being alone and unwanted.

T F 7. In facing death, the proposed sequence is: denial, anger, bargaining, depression, acceptance.

T F 8. Passive euthanasia is less of an ethical problem than active euthanasia is.

T F 9. The expression of emotion is typical of the intermediate phase of grief.

T F 10. Anticipatory grief can help prepare a person for the death of a spouse.

SELF TEST B

Circle the letter of the choice that completes each item.

1. According to Nagy, children tend to personify death when they are about the age of: (a) 2; (b) 4; (c) 7; (d) 13.

2. Karrie has been diagnosed as having leukemia. She feels sure that she will get better, but she says that she knows that right now she is sick all the time. Karrie's thinking about death is in Stage: (a) 1; (b) 3; (c) 4; (d) 5.

3. For adolescent populations, suicide: (a) is very rare; (b) has declined since peaking in 1968; (c) is increasing; (d) is employed by one out of three drug users.

4. The true realization of death and its certainty in middle age often leads to: (a) life review; (b) stability of life goals; (c) a feeling of satisfaction; (d) fear.

5. Among the elderly, suicide seems to be related to: (a) fear of further medical ailments; (b) a sense of loss; (c) brain atrophy; (d) psychosis.

6. Lorraine is dying of cancer. At age 47 she feels she has been dealt an unbearably unjust blow. She seems to hate everyone around her and is making life nearly unbearable for her husband, doctors, and nurses. Kübler-Ross would say that Lorraine is in the stage of: (a) denial; (b) anger; (c) depression; (d) acceptance.

7. Bob has been told of his rare and fatal blood disease. He has given up all hope of recovery and wants only to "die in peace." Bob is experiencing: (a) sociological death; (b) psychic death; (c) biological death; (d) physiological death.

8. A special institution set up to meet the needs of terminally ill patients is called: (a) Make Today Count; (b) the Shanti Project; (c) a moratorium; (d) a hospice.

9. The emotional response to death is called: (a) bereavement; (b) mourning; (c) grief; (d) thane.

10.   Taking opportunities, before death actually occurs, to practice showing the emotions that will arise when a spouse dies is
called: (a) anticipatory grief; (b) grief therapy; (c) morbid
grief; (d) bereavement.

VIGNETTES

1.   During adolescence, the topic of death is a popular subject of
"rap" sessions. After reading Chapter 18, what do you think would
be some major differences in any discussion of death conducted by
adolescents as compared to a similar discussion by adults?

2.   Often, when friends and relatives visit terminally ill patients,
they are very uncomfortable. They make "small talk" and purpose-
fully avoid discussion of medical conditions or death. What would
you do in the same situation?

ANSWER KEY
_____

CHAPTER 1

Self Test A

1. a (p. 4)
2. a (p. 5)
3. d (p. 11)
4. b (p. 12)
5. c (pp. 13-14)

6. b (p. 17)
7. c (p. 19)
8. a (p. 22)
9. d (p. 32)
10. b (pp. 36-37)

Completion

1. quantitative, qualitative
   (p. 4)
2. individual differences
   (p. 11)
3. critical period (p. 12)
4. proximodistal (p. 12)
5. Mechanistic, Organismic
   (pp. 13-16)

6. nature-nurture (p. 21)
7. naturalistic, normative (p. 29)
8. baby biographies (p. 29)
9. independent, dependent (p. 31)
10. self-fulfilling prophecy
    (pp. 30-31)

True-False

1. T (p. 4)
2. F (p. 4)
3. F (p. 8)

4. T (p. 11)
5. T (p. 12)
6. F (p. 14)

275

7. F (pp. 16-17)   9. F (p. 31)
8. T (p. 18)   10. T (p. 33)

Word Scramble

1. TABULA RASA (p. 14)   6. PHALLIC (p. 16)
2. LONGITUDINAL (p. 33)   7. PREMORAL (p. 16)
3. CEPHALOCAUDAL (p. 12)   8. SCHIZOPHRENIA (p. 28)
4. CLASSICAL (p. 13)   9. COHORT (p. 34)
5. ORGANISMIC (p. 14)   10. INFORMED CONSENT (pp. 36-37)

LIFE SPAN (pp. 7-8)

Self Test B

1. d (pp. 11-12)   6. b (pp. 19-20)
2. b (p. 13)   7. c (p. 22)
3. c (pp. 16-17)   8. b (p. 30)
4. a (p. 17)   9. a (p. 34)
5. d (p. 19)   10. c (p. 38)

Vignettes

1. The nature-nurture controversy is the basis of Pygmalion. The position of the professor is clearly mechanistic. He holds to a tabula rasa notion that Liza has been shaped by her environment and can thus be reshaped. Your friend's preformationist view is the other extreme and you might argue for a middle-ground organismic perspective.

2. The Industrial Revolution, need for increasing education, social concerns for child welfare, and adults' increasing feelings of responsibility for how children turn out are all advances that have culminated in our current "child centered" culture.

3. You should require clear experimental evidence as the only effective way to demonstrate a causal relationship. To say that children who watch violent TV are themselves more violent is not adequate evidence. Such data are correlational and show a relationship between TV and child violence but do not show cause-effect. It may well be, for example, that violent children prefer more-violent shows rather than violent shows teaching violence to children.

CHAPTER 2

Self Test A

1. c (p. 44)   6. a (p. 59)
2. b (p. 47)   7. c (p. 60)
3. c (p. 48)   8. b (p. 68)
4. d (p. 51)   9. c (pp. 72-73)
5. a (p. 54)   10. b (p. 74)

Completion

1. sperm, egg, Fallopian tube, zygote (p. 44)
2. chromosomes, autosomes, sex chromosomes (pp. 46-47)
3. homozygous, heterozygous (p. 48)
4. independent segregation (p. 51)
5. Down's syndrome (p. 52)
6. Barr body (p. 54)
7. Klinefelter's syndrome, testosterone (p. 54)
8. germinal, embryonic disk, placenta, umbilical cord, amniotic sac (pp. 59-60)
9. spontaneous abortion, trimester (p. 63)
10. fetal alcohol syndrome (p. 68)

Term Finder

```
A  J  O  Q  U  L  T  R  A  S  O  U  N  D  M  P
E  L  V  U  I  S  M  O  D  E  R  A  P  E  R  P
D  W  L  A  X  I  N  D  G  Y  T  E  S  E  L  B
G  O  G  E  O  Q  N  A  E  R  A  S  E  C  C  M
E  M  Y  U  L  U  C  V  C  P  S  D  A  T  O  O
N  S  O  L  M  S  R  E  N  R  U  T  I  O  D  D
A  G  N  I  N  E  K  C  I  U  Q  V  X  D  I  B
K  A  S  S  X  O  N  W  I  E  T  T  B  E  Y  I
A  M  N  I  O  C  E  N  T  E  S  I  S  R  E  P
R  O  M  T  I  B  K  C  L  Y  Q  S  S  M  O  F
Y  S  R  O  C  D  L  K  C  M  V  I  L  T  L  A
O  L  E  V  G  Y  N  O  S  P  E  R  M  A  I  L
T  E  T  N  A  F  T  S  E  F  K  O  M  X  G  J
Y  A  E  D  B  S  M  J  N  L  F  X  O  I  T  O
P  E  R  A  A  N  J  X  E  L  M  N  N  D  H  L
E  F  P  L  S  D  O  I  G  O  A  N  N  F  G  E
P  R  B  V  T  H  A  L  I  D  O  M  I  D  E  C
```

True-False

1. T (p. 48)
2. F (p. 48)
3. F (p. 59)
4. T (pp. 57-58)
5. F (p. 75)
6. F (p. 68)

277

7. T (p. 73)
8. T (p. 67)

9. T (p. 73)
10. F (p. 77)

Self Test B

1. c (p. 44)
2. b (p. 50)
3. b (p. 46)
4. b (p. 47)
5. b (p. 47)

6. c (pp. 75-77)
7. a (p. 47)
8. b (p. 60)
9. b (p. 59)
10. a (p. 74)

CHAPTER 3

Self Test A

1. b (p. 84)
2. c (p. 84)
3. a (p. 85)
4. a (p. 86)
5. c (p. 88)

6. a (p. 89)
7. a (p. 97)
8. b (p. 97)
9. c (p. 101)
10. a (p. 104)

Completion

1. neonatal (p. 84)
2. twenty, seven (p. 84)
3. lanugo, vernix caseosa (p. 84)
4. fontanels (p. 84)
5. Apgar scale, appearance, pulse, grimace, activity, respiration (pp. 84-85)

6. see, hear, smell, taste (pp. 87-88)
7. first (p. 92)
8. reflex behaviors, subcortical (p. 97)
9. scooting (p. 98)
10. maturational (pp. 103-104)

Matching

1. i (p. 84)
2. j (p. 84)
3. f (p. 88)
4. h (p. 86)
5. g (p. 86)

6. c (p. 87)
7. a (p. 87)
8. d (p. 107)
9. e (p. 95)
10. b (pp. 95-96)

True-False

1. T (p. 84)	9. T (p. 97)
2. F (p. 85)	10. T (p. 103)
3. F (p. 85)	11. T (p. 98)
4. T (p. 86)	12. T (pp. 100-101)
5. F (pp. 87-88)	13. F (p. 102)
6. F (pp. 90-91)	14. F (pp. 104-106)
7. F (pp. 93-94)	15. T (p. 106)
8. T (p. 96)	

Self Test B

1. c (p. 92)	6. b (p. 104)
2. c (p. 86)	7. a (p. 97)
3. b (p. 102)	8. b (p. 98)
4. a (p. 103)	9. c (pp. 104-105)
5. c (p. 94)	10. b (p. 107)

Vignettes

1.   You could briefly describe the transitional nature of the neo-natal period, indicating that preterm infants have more difficulty at this time.   Then review the data by the American Academy of Pediatrics on infant care and data from Iran on retardation of motor development, and Gesell (1924), Zelazo, Zelazo, and Kolb (1972) on acceleration of motor development.   Your conclusion should be cautious but positive that special programs could be effective in helping preterm infants.

2.   Infants' sensory systems are functional, though immature, at birth.   Review the data on depth and visual preference behavior as well as other sensory systems.

3.   You should advise that breast feeding does have distinct nutri-tional value over bottle feeding but that the mother's attitude is really crucial.   A mother should never be forced into breast feed-ing or feel guilty about bottle feeding.   The quality of the mother-child relationship is what is crucial.

CHAPTER 4

Self Test A

1. c (p. 112)	6. c (p. 128)
2. b (p. 114)	7. a (p. 131)
3. c (p. 115)	8. d (p. 137)
4. a (p. 119)	9. b (pp. 137-138)
5. c (p. 122)	10. b (p. 144)

Completion

1. schema, assimilation, accommodation (pp. 112-113)
2. sensory, objects; permanent; goal-directed (p. 113)
3. secondary circular reaction (pp. 113-114)
4. conservation (p. 118)
5. learning (p. 119)
6. imitate (p. 120)
7. UCS, UCR, CS (p. 121)
8. one (pp. 122-123)
9. expressive jargon (p. 128)
10. Brazelton Behavioral Assessment, Cattel Infant Intelligence (pp. 138-139)

Matching

1. d (p. 112)
2. f (p. 112)
3. a (p. 114)
4. g (p. 119)
5. i (pp. 121-122)
6. b (pp. 123-124)
7. h (p. 128)
8. j (p. 128)
9. c (p. 131)
10. e (p. 132)

Self Test B

1. d (pp. 112-113)
2. b (pp. 117-119)
3. c (p. 113)
4. a (pp. 123-124)
5. c (p. 128)
6. a (p. 130)
7. b (p. 131)
8. d (p. 136)
9. a (p. 138)
10. c (pp. 144-145)

Vignettes

1. Angela is in the tertiary circular reaction stage and has an incomplete schema of object permanence. She is upset because for her the ball is, in part, being under the chair. When she doesn't find it there she thinks it no longer exists. Tell her mother that she just lost her ball and can't find it.

2. The Daleys have made things worse by giving Eric intermittent reinforcement for his tantrums. It would have been better to always give in. Now the task is more difficult. They should _always_ put Eric into a predetermined spot where he can't get hurt and not allow him out until _after_ he is quiet and then reward his quiet behavior.

3. Infant intelligence tests will not predict later intelligence and so the purpose of testing the infant is highly questionable. You might also ask how they know the child is "gifted" since early intelligence is based on sensory and motor development and not on verbal skills. Gifted how?

CHAPTER 5

Self Test A

1. b (p. 152)
2. b (p. 155)
3. a (p. 155)
4. c (p. 158)
5. a (pp. 158-159)

6. d (p. 161)
7. a (pp. 163-164)
8. c (p. 166)
9. c (p. 174)
10. a (p. 176)

Completion

1. love, rage, fear (p. 152)
2. basic rhythmic, anger, pain, frustration (p. 155)
3. anal (p. 158)
4. quality, quantity (p. 159)
5. nuclear, mother, mother-baby (pp. 159-160)

6. temperament (p. 160)
7. first (p. 163)
8. Attachment (p. 167)
9. hospitalism (p. 173)
10. separation anxiety, protest, despair, detachment (p. 174)

True-False

1. F (p. 152)
2. T (p. 155)
3. T (p. 158)
4. F (p. 159)
5. T (p. 162)

6. F (p. 163)
7. T (pp. 164-165)
8. F (pp. 166-167)
9. T (p. 168)
10. F (p. 175)

Word Scramble

1. RHYTHMIC (p. 155)
2. CATHECT (p. 158)
3. ORAL (p. 158)
4. IMPRINTING (p. 160)
5. ATTACHMENT (p. 167)

6. STRANGER (p. 170)
7. HOSPITALISM (p. 173)
8. PROTEST (p. 174)
9. ENGROSSMENT (p. 176)
10. SOCIOMETRY (p. 180)

TEMPERAMENT (p. 160)

Self Test B

1. a (p. 155)
2. c (p. 156)
3. b (p. 159
4. c (p. 161)
5. a (pp. 163-164)

6. a (p. 160)
7. b (p. 163)
8. c (p. 167)
9. d (p. 169)
10. c (p. 174)

Vignettes

1. Since the infant's "social signals" of smiling or vocalizations may go unnoticed, it is important that the parents learn to use other senses to "read" the infant's messages. For example, different types of crying are often accompanied by different visually obvious cues such as breath-holding, becoming red-faced, and so on. The main problems will be communication ones.

2. A 2½-year-old may react negatively to such a situation for at least three reasons. First, a strong maternal/paternal attachment may, when broken, lead to such a response. Rooming in by one or both parents should help. Stranger anxiety may also be a factor, and a calm gradual introduction of pediatric staff and routines with a parent present should prove effective. Finally, the confinement and regimentation of hospitalization will frustrate the 2½-year-old's striving for autonomy. Give the child "important chores" to accomplish to help restore a sense of independence.

CHAPTER 6

Self Test A

1. a (p. 188)
2. b (p. 188)
3. b (p. 189)
4. c (p. 195)
5. d (p. 196)

6. a (pp. 196-197)
7. b (pp. 202-203)
8. a (p. 207)
9. a (pp. 209-210)
10. c (p. 213)

Completion

1. 2, 3, smaller, lighter (p. 188)
2. failure-to-thrive (p. 189)
3. physical abuse, accidents (p. 193)
4. physical force (p. 194)
5. psychotherapy, mother surrogates (p. 195)

6. signs, symbols (p. 196)
7. Deferred imitation (p. 196)
8. figural (p. 199)
9. age-grading, adult-child, higher (p. 201)
10. comprehensive, developmental day care, custodial child care (pp. 203-204)

Matching

1. o (p. 189)
2. i (p. 196)
3. n (p. 196)
4. m (p. 197)
5. e (p. 198)
6. f (p. 201)
7. h (p. 203)
8. k (p. 203)

9. a (p. 204)
10. b (pp. 203-204)
11. c (p. 207)
12. d (p. 207)
13. l (p. 207)
14. j (p. 209)
15. g (p. 214)

Self Test B

1. c (p. 189)
2. d (pp. 189-190)
3. c (p. 189)
4. a (p. 194)
5. c (p. 195)

6. b (p. 199)
7. c (p. 209)
8. d (pp. 201-202)
9. a (p. 203)
10. c (pp. 212-215)

Vignettes

1. Thumb sucking is more of a habit than an indicator of emotional stress. Assure the parents that breaking such a habit is a relatively straightforward matter if it doesn't first disappear by itself. Dental problems are rare unless sucking continues past age 5.

2. Children are just beginning to use symbolic function. Toys which allow the child to "exercise" the imagination are therefore excellent. Also, toys which provide opportunity for discovery and practice in specific skills such as seriation, classification, or language skills also are excellent. Finally, toys which allow the child to do something and then undo it will help the child discover reversibility.

3. Preschools which employ staff trained in child development, who break the children into small groups, and have a favorable child/staff ratio tend to be successful in helping children prepare for school. Emphasis on social development with cognitive advancement a corollary concern, will provide children with skills needed for both the social and academic worlds of school.

CHAPTER 7

Self Test A

1. a (p. 220)
2. a (p. 221)
3. b (p. 222)
4. b (p. 230)
5. d (p. 225)
6. c (pp. 227-230)
7. b (p. 241)
8. c (pp. 232-233)
9. a (p. 245)
10. c (p. 248)

Completion

1. Oedipus complex, Electra complex (p. 220)
2. introjection (p. 221)
3. initiative, guilt (p. 221)
4. Sex typing (p. 222)
5. biological, cultural (p. 223)
6. Psychoanalytic, social learning, socialization, observation, reciprocal role (p. 225)
7. more marked (pp. 227-228)
8. opposite, same sexed (p. 228)
9. Television (p. 230)
10. 2, 6 (p. 231)
11. activity by the children themselves (p. 232)
12. televised, tolerant (p. 235)
13. done to rather than doing, self-sufficiency (p. 237)
14. prosocial, altruistic (p. 237)
15. Authoritarian, Permissive, Authoritative (p. 241)

True-False

1. T (pp. 243-244)
2. T (pp. 245-246)
3. F (p. 247)
4. T (p. 248)
5. F (p. 220)
6. F (p. 221)

7. T (p. 222)
8. F (p. 227)

9. F (p. 223)
10. T (pp. 226-227)

Word Scramble

1. OEDIPUS (p. 220)
2. PHALLIC (p. 220)
3. PENIS (p. 220)
4. INTROJECTION (p. 221)
5. SOCIALIZATION (p. 225)

6. OBSERVATION (p. 225)
7. PASSIVITY (p. 237)
8. AUTHORITARIAN (p. 241)
9. AUTHORITATIVE (p. 241)
10. PARALLEL (p. 245)

INITIATIVE (p. 221)

Self Test B

1. a (p. 220)
2. b (p. 221)
3. c (p. 227)
4. b (pp. 227-228)
5. b (p. 231)

6. b (pp. 235-236)
7. c (pp. 239-241)
8. b (p. 241)
9. a (pp. 241-242)
10. d (p. 247)

Vignettes

1. Evidence partially supports your friend's statement that culture plays a crucial role. Yet some biological factors may also be rather important. Psychoanalytic, cognitive, and learning theory each place different emphasis on biological factors.

2. Ridicule, shame, and logic will have little or negative effect on Billy. Get him actively involved. Slowly get him to enter the bathroom, then the tub without water. Have him try to put things of various size down the drain until he discovers that there is no danger of his slipping in.

CHAPTER 8

Self Test A

1. a (p. 256)
2. a (p. 256)
3. b (p. 257)
4. c (p. 261)
5. d (p. 262)

6. a (p. 261)
7. b (p. 264)
8. b (p. 275)
9. c (p. 291)
10. b (pp. 298-299)

Completion

1. larger, nutrition (p. 256)
2. ossification, 18 (p. 256)
3. influence, pneumonia (p. 259)
4. accidents (p. 258)
5. running, jumping, throwing, kicking (pp. 260-261)
6. symbols, operations (p. 261)

7. realism (p. 262)
8. animism (p. 262)
9. artificialism (pp. 262-263)
10. fail to conserve, vacillate, reversibility, identity, compensation (p. 264)

Matching

1. g (p. 264)	6. h (pp. 277-278)
2. b (p. 269)	7. c (p. 280)
3. i (p. 269)	8. d (p. 281)
4. j (p. 265)	9. e (p. 283)
5. a (p. 275)	10. f (p. 288)

True-False

1. T (p. 258)	9. T (p. 279)
2. F (p. 262)	10. T (pp. 280-281)
3. T (p. 263)	11. T (pp. 282-284)
4. T (p. 264)	12. F (p. 285)
5. F (p. 265)	13. F (p. 288)
6. F (p. 269)	14. T (p. 291)
7. T (pp. 274-275)	15. T (p. 299)
8. F (p. 279)	

Self Test B

1. c (p. 256)	6. c (p. 262)
2. c (p. 259)	7. c (p. 265)
3. a (p. 260)	8. a (p. 269)
4. b (pp. 260-261)	9. c (p. 279)
5. a (p. 261)	10. a (p. 296)

Vignettes

1. It is true that there are differences between motor skills of boys and girls; however, these may well reflect more cultural expectations than innate abilities. Govatos (1959) presented data which indicate that boys and girls are so nearly equal that there is no reason to separate them for gym. Indeed, encouragement of girls' physical education may well result and this could greatly reduce male/female differences.

2. Despite social learning theory's predictions, the moral level of parents is not necessarily reflected by their offspring. Major theorists propose that cognitive development, not parental modeling, is the crucial ingredient for moral advancement. The child's behavior is controlled by a desire to avoid pain. When hunger pains occur, they motivate him to get food and risk the lesser pain of punishment for shoplifting. The Crenshaw's child is in Kohlberg's Stage 1 of moral reasoning and can be best assisted by a cognitive approach.

CHAPTER 9

Self Test A

1. a (p. 306)	2. c (p. 306)

3. b (p. 306)
4. d (pp. 308-310)
5. c (p. 312)
6. b (pp. 312-313)

7. c (pp. 313-314)
8. a (pp. 315-316)
9. a (p. 318)
10. c (p. 327)

Completion

1. latency (p. 306)
2. regress (p. 306)
3. productivity (p. 306)
4. peer, parent (p. 312)
5. adaptable, conforming (p. 312)
6. apathy, aggression (pp. 313-314)

7. self-image (p. 317)
8. identification, skills, accomplishments (p. 319)
9. older girls (p. 324)
10. fathers, mothers, fathers, same-sex (p. 324)

True-False

1. T (p. 306)
2. T (p. 309)
3. F (p. 311)
4. F (p. 312)
5. T (pp. 315-316)

6. T (p. 318)
7. F (p. 319)
8. T (p. 324)
9. T (p. 327)
10. F (pp. 328-330)

Word Scramble

1. REGRESSION (p. 306)
2. INFERIORITY (p. 306)
3. SOCIOGRAM (p. 312)
4. VIRTUE (p. 318)
5. VICARIOUS (p. 320)

6. ENURESIS (p. 332)
7. ANXIETY (p. 334)
8. HYPERKINESIS (p. 330)
9. SUPPORTIVE (p. 336)
10. PLACEBO (p. 331)

INFANTILE AUTISM (p. 334)

Self Test B

1. b (p. 306)
2. c (p. 306)
3. c (pp. 307-308)
4. b (p. 312)
5. a (p. 314)

6. c (p. 319)
7. b (p. 324)
8. a (p. 320)
9. c (p. 330)
10. b (p. 336)

Vignettes

1. Since popular children are generally healthy and attractive you would want to include steps to maximize Harold's physical appearance. Social-skills training in being poised and confident, but not overbearing, would be a crucial element. Finally, you would want to work to give Harold a moderate level of positive self-regard.

2. Whether a mother works or not is not crucial for a child so long as the home atmosphere is one of love, acceptance, and respect.

Since Mrs. Smith enjoys her job, giving it up may cause resentment and a feeling of uselessness. She should keep her job and concentrate on the quality, not the quantity, of her mother-child interactions.

CHAPTER 10

Self Test A

1. c (p. 344)	6. c (pp. 349-350)
2. a (p. 344)	7. d (p. 350)
3. b (p. 345)	8. b (p. 352)
4. b (p. 346)	9. b (p. 358)
5. a (pp. 348-349)	10. c (p. 361)

Completion

1. Pubescence, puberty (p. 344)
2. menarche (p. 344)
3. adolescent growth spurt (p. 346)
4. secular (p. 345)
5. sebaceous (p. 347)
6. physical appearance (pp. 348-349)
7. early, late (pp. 349-350)
8. anorexia nervosa (p. 350)
9. 16, qualitative (p. 353)
10. personal fable (p. 354)

Matching

1. i (p. 344)	6. g (p. 347)
2. b (p. 344)	7. j (p. 352)
3. h (p. 364)	8. c (p. 354)
4. a (p. 345)	9. d (p. 354)
5. e (p. 347)	10. f (p. 362)

True-False

1. F (p. 344)	6. F (p. 348)
2. T (pp. 349-350)	7. F (p. 351)
3. F (p. 346)	8. T (p. 352)
4. T (p. 346)	9. F (p. 358)
5. F (p. 348)	10. T (p. 363)

Self Test B

1. c (p. 344)	6. a (p. 348)
2. a (p. 344)	7. a (p. 352)
3. c (p. 364)	8. a (p. 355)
4. d (pp. 346-348)	9. b (p. 357)
5. a (p. 347)	10. c (p. 353)

Vignettes

1. Mary is exhibiting a peculiar form of adolescent egocentrism, the personal fable. Explain that the occurrence of cognitive limitations in young adolescents is not unusual and that Mary is

accurately reporting her view of the world.

2. Vocational choices tend to reflect the adolescent's socio-economic status, sex, parental attitudes, and schooling. You would certainly consider these factors along with the personality of the individual.

CHAPTER 11

Self Test A

1. b (p. 370)
2. d (p. 370)
3. d (p. 372)
4. b (p. 371)
5. a (p. 377)

6. b (p. 381)
7. b (p. 383)
8. a (p. 393)
9. c (p. 396)
10. a (p. 389)

Completion

1. contradictory, vacillating (p. 370)
2. genital stage (p. 371)
3. identity, role confusion (p. 371)
4. know, like, respect (p. 374)
5. same (p. 376)

6. abstract, particular (p. 380)
7. involuntary, retarded, capable (p. 391)
8. status offender (p. 395)
9. hostile, indifferent, affectionate (pp. 396-397)
10. women (p. 385)

True-False

1. F (p. 370)
2. T (p. 372)
3. T (p. 376)
4. F (p. 381)
5. F (p. 382)

6. F (p. 385)
7. T (p. 388)
8. T (pp. 389-390)
9. F (p. 391)
10. F (p. 392)

Word Scramble

1. LIBIDO (p. 371)
2. GENITAL (p. 371)
3. INTELLECTUALISM (p. 371)
4. ASCETICISM (p. 371)
5. ACHIEVEMENT (p. 372)

6. FORECLOSURE (p. 372)
7. MORATORIUM (p. 372)
8. CAPABLE (p. 391)
9. SIMILARITY (p. 378)

CHAUVINISM (p. 376)

Self Test B

1. a (p. 371)
2. d (p. 371)
3. c (p. 371)
4. d (p. 376)
5. a (p. 378)

6. b (p. 386)
7. d (pp. 387-388)
8. b (p. 389)
9. a (p. 393)
10. a (p. 394)

1. Probably three major points should be included in your address: (a) Parents should try communicating all along, not just during adolescence, and this should include sexual matters as a legitimate topic. (b) Parents should realize that most disagreements reflect concerns over timing rather than issues. (c) Adolescents vacillate between dependency and independence and cannot be expected to be totally consistent. Patience, understanding, and guidance are needed in large doses.

2. Regardless of who teaches adolescents about sexuality, it is important that it be done early since adolescents mature earlier now and initiate sexual activity earlier. Also, emphasis on the emotional and cognitive view of the adolescents is crucial. If the personal fable persists, all the factual information in the world about conception and contraception will have no effect. The teen-agers will say "Yes, but not me!" The crucial questions go beyond who and include when and how!

CHAPTER 12

Self Test A

1. c (p. 406)	6. d (p. 416)
2. a (p. 407)	7. d (p. 417)
3. b (pp. 410-411)	8. a (p. 418)
4. b (pp. 412-413)	9. c (pp. 419-420)
5. b (p. 414)	10. a (p. 420)

Completion

1. muscular strength, senses (p. 407)
2. 30, females, males, accidents (p. 407)
3. premenstrual, menstrual, hormones (pp. 410-412)
4. Fluid, decline (p. 412)
5. crystallized, increase (pp. 412-413)
6. more, social interactions, neurological (p. 414)
7. emotional (p. 414)
8. critical event (p. 417)
9. fear of success (p. 420)
10. Dual-career, increasing (p. 421)

Matching

1. e (p. 407)	6. g (p. 416)
2. f (p. 407)	7. i (p. 416)
3. d (p. 412)	8. j (p. 417)
4. a (p. 412)	9. b (p. 421)
5. h (p. 413)	10. c (p. 420)

True-False

1. F (p. 407)
2. T (p. 408)
3. F (p. 408)
4. T (p. 412)
5. F (p. 413)

6. T (pp. 415-416)
7. F (p. 416)
8. F (pp. 418-419)
9. F (p. 420)
10. F (p. 421)

Self Test B

1. a (p. 407)
2. c (p. 407)
3. b (pp. 408-409)
4. b (p. 411)
5. a (p. 412)

6. b (p. 414)
7. d (p. 416)
8. a (pp. 417-418)
9. a (p. 420)
10. b (p. 421)

Vignettes

1. College women need to be convinced that it is "OK to succeed." The inclusion of female professors to serve as role models would be a very valuable step. Another possible step might be to provide awareness seminars to acquaint women with professionals who are female and to heighten awareness of cultural blocks that exist.

2. Your friend needs to know that young adults, who are physically and mentally at the peak of human development, make excellent music students. While manual dexterity does decline in adulthood it is a slight decline that is more than compensated for by the adults' increased motivation.

CHAPTER 13

Self Test A

1. c (p. 426)
2. b (p. 427)
3. d (p. 429)
4. a (p. 435)
5. a (p. 436)

6. a (p. 437)
7. a (p. 440)
8. b (p. 446)
9. a (p. 455)
10. d (p. 449)

Completion

1. careers, personality (p. 428)
2. Buhler, self-fulfillment (p. 426)
3. intimacy, isolation, mutual orgasm, procreation (p. 427)
4. 20's, religion, social class (pp. 434-435)

5. conflict-habituated, total (pp. 436-437)
6. total (p. 436)
7. cohabitating, increasing (p. 443)
8. parenthood (p. 444)
9. disengagement (p. 449)
10. adjustment (p. 455)

True-False

1. T (p. 426)
2. F (pp. 427-432)
3. T (p. 433)
4. F (p. 434)
5. T (p. 435)

6. T (p. 437)
7. F (p. 437)
8. T (pp. 450-451)
9. T (pp. 441-442)
10. F (p. 456)

Self Test B

1. a (p. 426)
2. b (p. 427)
3. d (p. 431)
4. d (p. 433)
5. b (p. 432)

6. d (pp. 434-435)
7. a (p. 436)
8. a (p. 440)
9. c (p. 450)
10. b (pp. 454-455)

Vignettes

1. The typical college student is fairly secure in general identity but is just beginning to narrow down his goals to be more specific about career, marriage, sex, and so on. He is fully mature physically and enjoys a robustness that many would envy. For all his development, however, many important decisions still lie before him.

2. Opinions on this issue will vary markedly. Violence and its acceptance of society at large, could be mentioned as a possible contributing factor. Poor economic conditions, unrealistic expectations for marriage, the lack of training in verbal communication and interpersonal social skills in childhood, and a family history of violence from generation to generation are also possible factors.

CHAPTER 14

Self Test A

1. b (p. 464)
2. d (p. 465)
3. b (p. 466)
4. a (p. 467)
5. c (pp. 467-468)

6. d (p. 468)
7. b (p. 469)
8. a (p. 470)
9. c (p. 471)
10. b (p. 473)

Completion

1. 40, 65, reevaluation (p. 463)
2. minor, Men, women (pp. 463-466)
3. complex, experience (p. 468)
4. climacteric (p. 466)
5. estrogen, testosterone (pp. 466-467)

6. different (p. 462)
7. double standard (p. 468)
8. increase, mid-fifties (p. 469)
9. conservation, formal operations (p. 470)
10. continuing education (p. 472)

1. T (p. 462)
2. F (p. 464)
3. T (p. 465)
4. F (p. 467)
5. F (p. 466)

6. T (p. 467)
7. F (pp. 468-469)
8. F (pp. 469-471)
9. T (p. 471)
10. F (p. 473)

Word Scramble

1. LIFE STRUCTURE (p. 473)
2. CLIMACTERIC (p. 466)
3. ESTROGEN (p. 466)
4. CRYPTOCHANGER (p. 473)
5. CREATIVITY (p. 471)

6. PERSISTER (p. 473)
7. PSEUDOCHANGER (p. 473)
8. COMPLEX (p. 468)
9. DOUBLD STANDARD (pp. 468-469)
10. FORMAL (p. 470)

MIDDLE AGE (p. 463)

Self Test B

1. c (p. 462)
2. d (p. 464)
3. b (p. 465)
4. a (p. 466)
5. c (p. 467)

6. d (pp. 468-469)
7. a (p. 469)
8. c (p. 473)
9. c (p. 473)
10. b (p. 474)

Vignettes

1. Your father's concern is easily understood. You might disagree that your mother's condition is due to menopause, in that her symptoms are not directly due to hormonal changes but rather are more a reflection of concern over the process of aging. Since the symptoms are not biological givens, there are things your father might do to help reduce them; for example, a short weekend vacation for "just the two of them" to help reassure your mother that she's not getting just older but better.

2. You might expect your clients to be around age 40 to 50. They may be seeking new employment because of a chronic incapacity for steady employment. If they are shifting to a new vocation, you can anticipate that their reasons will vary considerably. They may have just seen their last offspring "out of the nest," they may have financial worries, or they may be experiencing some anxiety in their present job. Major concerns will be to encourage the clients to be retrained, to help them to recognize the possibilities that are open, and to aid them in making the most of their potential.

CHAPTER 15

Self Test A

1. c (p. 478)
2. a (p. 478)

3. c (pp. 479-480)
4. d (p. 480)

5. b (p. 481)
6. d (p. 482)
7. b (pp. 482-483)

8. c (pp. 483-484)
9. c (p. 486)
10. b (p. 492)

Completion

1. favorably (p. 478)
2. family, job (p. 483)
3. generativity, stagnate (pp. 479-480)
4. wisdom, socializing, sexual-izing, flexibility, mental (p. 480)

5. Buhler (p. 480)
6. Introversion (p. 482)
7. off-time (p. 483)
8. midlife crisis, stability (pp. 484-485)
9. white, healthy (p. 489)
10. disenchantment (p. 492)

Matching

1. f (p. 479)
2. c (p. 480)
3. e (p. 480)
4. i (p. 485)
5. d (p. 487)

6. a (pp. 487-488)
7. j (p. 492)
8. h (p. 492)
9. b (p. 494)
10. g (p. 495)

True-False

1. T (p. 478)
2. T (p. 481)
3. T (p. 492)
4. F (p. 492)
5. T (pp. 483-484)

6. F (pp. 486-487)
7. T (pp. 487-488)
8. F (p. 489)
9. F (pp. 493-494)
10. T (p. 496)

Self Test B

1. a (p. 480)
2. c (p. 480)
3. b (p. 484)
4. c (p. 484)
5. c (pp. 485-486)

6. b (pp. 487-488)
7. d (p. 488)
8. d (p. 489)
9. b (pp. 492)
10. c (pp. 494)

Vignettes

1. You might begin by reminding your audience that midlife is called the prime of life. Report that self-concept in this period is quite high, that middle-agers enjoy power and competence on the job, and that they seldom suffer from the self-doubt and lack of effectiveness found in adolescence and young adulthood because they have a storehouse of life experience from which to draw. There are problems in midlife, to be sure, but there are problems and chal-lenges in all life-span periods. Middle-aged people report that they are pretty well satisfied with their lot, and well they should be.

2. Marriage in the middle years involves changes in the partners that will probably change, possibly for the better, the

relationship. The slight decline in sexual functioning may be troublesome, and a counselor needs to emphasize that cultural expectations should not be allowed to create further difficulty. There will also be the mismatch between the man and woman in their views on aging, their self-concept, and their level of happiness. Enabling the partners to understand these views will need to be a central goal of counseling.

CHAPTER 16

Self Test A

1. c (p. 504)
2. c (p. 505)
3. b (p. 507)
4. d (pp. 508-509)
5. b (pp. 509-510)

6. a (p. 511)
7. c (p. 513)
8. b (p. 515)
9. a (pp. 517-519)
10. a (p. 521)

Completion

1. negative, ageism (p. 504)
2. Gerontology, increasing (p. 504)
3. young-old, old-old (p. 505)
4. senescence, physical (p. 505)
5. primary, secondary (p. 507)

6. declining, heart disease, cancer, stroke (p. 508)
7. slowdown (p. 511)
8. error (p. 514)
9. terminal drop (p. 522)
10. short-term, long-term (p. 524)

Matching

1. h (p. 506)
2. a (p. 508)
3. g (p. 510)
4. c (p. 513)
5. d (p. 513)
6. i (p. 514)

7. b (p. 516)
8. l (p. 519)
9. k (pp. 521-522)
10. e (p. 524)
11. f (p. 524)
12. j (p. 519)

Word Scramble

1. AGEISM (p. 504)
2. GERONTOLOGY (p. 504)
3. GERIATRICS (p. 504)
4. SENESCENCE (p. 505)
5. PRIMARY (p. 507)

6. SECONDARY (p. 507)
7. SENILITY (p. 515)
8. ALZHEIMER (p. 516)
9. COMPETENCE (p. 518)
10. CROSS-SEQUENTIAL (p. 519)

TERMINAL DROP (p. 522)

Self Test B

1. a (p. 506)
2. b (p. 505)
3. c (p. 507)
4. c (p. 514)
5. b (p. 518)

6. c (p. 522)
7. d (p. 518)
8. a (p. 525)
9. a (pp. 524-525)
10. c (pp. 529-531)

CHAPTER 17

Self Test A

1. c (p. 536)	6. d (p. 540)
2. b (p. 541)	7. c (p. 540)
3. a (p. 538)	8. c (pp. 543-544)
4. b (p. 539)	9. a (p. 545)
5. a (p. 540)	10. d (p. 562)

Completion

1. self-esteem (p. 536)
2. activity, Disengagement (p. 538)
3. mature, armored, rocking-chair (p. 540)
4. reorganizers, focused, disengaged, unintegrated (p. 540)
5. ego-integrity, despair (p. 543)
6. ego-transcendence, body transcendence (p. 544)
7. women, men (p. 550)
8. surrogate, distant (p. 554)
9. poverty (p. 558)
10. minority, Social Security (p. 562)

True-False

1. F (p. 538)	9. T (p. 551)
2. T (p. 539)	10. T (p. 552)
3. F (p. 540)	11. T (p. 553)
4. T (p. 544)	12. F (p. 553)
5. T (p. 544)	13. T (p. 554)
6. F (p. 545)	14. T (pp. 556-557)
7. F (pp. 547-548)	15. F (p. 559)
8. F (pp. 549-550)	

Word Scramble

1. ACTIVITY (p. 538)
2. SOLITARY (p. 538)
3. BREAKDOWN (p. 539)
4. APATHETIC (p. 541)
5. DESPAIR (p. 543)
6. EGO-DIFFERENTIATION (pp. 543-544)
7. INDEPENDENCE (p. 553)
8. FORMAL (p. 554)
9. POVERTY (p. 558)
10. COMMUNITY (p. 559)

SELF-ESTEEM (p. 541)

Self Test B

1. c (p. 539)	6. a (pp. 549-550)
2. a (p. 540)	7. c (p. 554)
3. c (p. 543)	8. b (pp. 558-559)
4. c (p. 544)	9. b (p. 551)
5. a (pp. 547-548)	10. d (p. 558)

Vignette

1. Everything you learned in Chapter 17 can bear on this issue.
The "bottom line" is that what constitutes the "proper" behavior for
your roommate's grandparents is for them to decide, not anyone else.
Self-esteem, the most important component of successful aging, is
best served by allowing the old to control their own lives. Contrary to activity theory, to which your roommate ascribes, being
busy is not necessarily being a "good" old person. This is particularly true if the people involved have tended to be rather passive
all their lives. You might point out that having a few close
friends is a common pattern for all adults. Tell your roommate that
the grandparent of today wants most of all for younger people to
"let me be me."

CHAPTER 18

Self Test A

1. b (p. 570)	6. a (p. 584)
2. c (p. 572)	7. b (p. 588)
3. a (p. 575)	8. a (p. 592)
4. d (p. 579)	9. b (pp. 592-593)
5. d (p. 583)	10. a (p. 577)

Matching

1. g (p. 571)	6. i (pp. 584-585)
2. d (p. 570)	7. h (p. 591)
3. j (p. 575)	8. e (p. 585)
4. b (p. 582)	9. f (p. 587)
5. a (p. 583)	10. c (p. 593)

True-False

1. T (p. 570)	6. T (pp. 579-580)
2. T (p. 571)	7. T (pp. 582-583)
3. F (p. 572)	8. F (p. 588)
4. T (p. 576)	9. T (p. 593)
5. F (p. 577)	10. T (p. 592)

Self Test B

1. c (p. 571)	6. b (p. 582)
2. b (p. 573)	7. b (p. 585)
3. c (p. 578)	8. d (p. 590)
4. a (p. 576)	9. c (p. 592)
5. b (pp. 580-581)	10. a (p. 592)

Vignettes

1. Such discussions during adolescence tend to be very abstract and depersonalized. Death is seen as a remote state that "could never happen to me" and thus adolescents tend to talk about "it." Middle-aged adults, however, have truly realized the certainty of their own death. They are engaged in life review and readjustment of life goals with the full realization of a finite amount of time remaining. Their discussions are, therefore, personalized and more concrete. They will include not only abstract philosophies of death but practical implications such as funerals, wills, and the like.

2. Hopefully, you would not avoid talking about what concerns the terminal patient the most, but you would not push the matter if he or she did not feel like discussing it. You would have to be sensitive to the stage in which the person might be in dealing with death, and this alone might dictate how you might act. Death is a very important event, and your refusal to talk about it if the patient wants to deprives him or her of an opportunity to grieve his or her own losses and to work through this last developmental event.

NOTES

NOTES

NOTES

NOTES

NOTES

NOTES